RESURGIUS REDUX

the sex war

Copyright © 2024 by E.M. Schorb. All rights reserved.

ISBN: 979-8-218-45094-6

Cover Design: Selah Bunzey

I do not wish women to have power over men; but over themselves.

—*Mary Wollstonecraft*

Politics, as the word is commonly understood, are nothing but corruptions.

—*Jonathan Swift*

RESURGIUS REDUX

the sex war

E.M. Schorb

HILL HOUSE   NEW YORK

Dedicated

to

Amanda Quaint Bering-Strait

and to

Juanna Donna Lorca,

without whose help, forbearance,

and little Red Diablos,

I could not have written this great work

TO THE READER

Serge Bering-Strait here. I have just finished reading Resurgius, *E.M. Schorb's account of my life to date, and am amazed at the degree of intimacy he has achieved in it. It appears that he has been my Doppelgänger, my vademecum—I blush to say it—present even at those sacred intimate moments when I was with my beloved Amanda.*

Greenwich Village gossip has it that he is an almost blind bard, who looks out at the world through large horn-rimmed glasses very like mine, very darkly, but perhaps those who say so are having me on, which is N.Y.U. slang for kidding. As Schorb has accurately described them, my mother and aunts, the sum total of the sad family I was born into, are clinicians of emotion, shallow of human feeling, only passionate in their desire to make themselves known to the ochlocracy and to tell it how to live—but certainly not to share the world with it. As for their attitude toward me, the young person in their midst, they take me for a nerdy and pimply adolescent. They ignore my genius-level I.Q. at their peril. Resurgius Redux *is my response to their ignorance of the real me.*

Justice is mine!

                    S.B. I *am* Resurgius.

1

THE UPRISING OF THE DONGS

Miz Mandalay, a magnificent Amazon of twenty-five with splendidly developed anti-sex objects, held a Doctorate in Liberal Tyranny from the University of Xantippe, where she had written an eyebrow-raising thesis, later published on Say-screen, in which she had daringly attempted to show that certain ancient Dongs, despite their obvious sexual swinishness, had manifested symptoms of emerging mental capacity, and had even been capable—and this is what had shocked the world—of a kind of tenderness.

Had the slum-lord class not become more liberal, that thesis might have consigned Miz Mandalay to the lower levels of governance. But these were turbulent times. It had become possible to say the un-sayable of ten years before. Dongs were cracking the information barrier, seeking a newer world, speaking boldly out from their hiding places, demanding Dong suffrage and other outrageous rights. Perhaps the most threatening of these revolutionary Dongs was a Spartacus-like character called Resurgius, known for his Tarzan-like physique, poetic speech, and flirtatious nature.

Whereas, after the Great Succession, the Dongs were content to be allowed to walk in the gutters, with their heads hanging, and manifesting upon demand every sign of shame, from reddening cheeks to the squeezing of the legs together, today they went about right on the sidewalks, and mingled with the Mize (though they were not generally allowed to address them unless spoken to); and of late small, radical groups of Dongs had been making open protest. Some had gone so far as to lift a leg and ask for the vote! (Not that the vote meant anything, even to the Mize; but the *idea*!)

To liberals of Miz Mandalay's persuasion, these indications of unrest among the once shamefaced Dong population were healthy signs, showing that today's was a healthy, vital society. Some, like Miz Mandalay herself, would give the Dongs the vote. She, being an inner council member, knew that the vote was merely symbolic, but she also knew that that was precisely what made it important. She would liken it to a valve from which to release the steam of frustration from the pressure-cooker of society. After all, she told herself, the Dongs *are* human beings, even if they are Dongs.

Miz Jaye Edgahoova, and others of conservative persuasion, felt differently. As Miz Edgahoova, a poco-porcine middle-aged Miz, put it: "These Dong protesters are highly dangerous, potentially. Let us recall that our own Movement started in protest. And let us remember, further, that in the antique days protest did no real good for us. It is not in the nature of power to give itself away. Most of you are too young to remember, but we who date back to the time before the Great Succession, do—that we used to say, *This is a Dong-dominated society*. Of course, what we young innocent vaginal revolutionaries did not understand at the time was how right we were. In those days, what we were naively doing was *asking* Dongs to stop dominating us and to empower us. It never seemed to occur to us that the fact that they *did* dominate indicated that they *could*—indeed, had, always. Why? Because dominance, after all, *is* power. And you cannot *ask* that the powerful cease being powerful. How can they stop being what they are? No, we came to realize that we couldn't simply ask for power—power is something you have to *take.* If you can take it, you are powerful; and if you can hold it, you remain powerful.

"Now today's liberals, the Dong fellow travellers, are asking us to give and give. Give in on this point, give in on that. Give in, and let the Dongs have the vote. Remember, that was the very first mistake the Dongs themselves made. That was the step that led to the Great Succession. The tactic in those days was to make the Dongs feel ashamed of their strength. We were successful in doing just that. Only through demoralizing the Dongs, only by making them feel ashamed of what they were, did we succeed in preparing them psychologically for the Great Capitulation which led to the Great Succession. Why, in shame, Charles Atlas himself—famous for kicking sand in people's faces at the beach—

became Charlotte Atlas and was thenceforth admired for the Grable-like beauty of her legs, or so it is claimed. And now persons like Miz Mandalay, perhaps unwittingly, with the same kind of misguided generosity of spirit that led to the downfall of the Dongs, are doing to us what we did years ago in Pre-Succession days to the Dongs.

"Those who aid subversives, even unwittingly, are themselves subversive, and enemies of the State. If Miz Mandalay were to achieve full control, I have no doubt but that she would turn Atalanta over to the Dongs. Do I detect the odor of the sexual regressive? That's why we must be vigilant, and at the same time take strong action on both fronts—against traitors, and against Dongs." She addressed the Emergency Session of the Univacual Council, with a special word for Miz Mandalay:

"And I suppose you would give in to their demands, Miz Mandalay, and then when the Dongs ask for the right to be delegates you'd give in again—and why not just save us all a great deal of time and turn the hard-won reins of governnesting over to them right now, I ask you? Why don't we just go back to jock strap rule—back to the rule of, please pardon my language—toxic masculine principle, pure ugly Sandowism—where war is peace? Hey?

Answer me that!" She twirled a not completely imaginary mustache and looked contemptuously at Miz Mandalay.

"If Miz Edgahoova were any kind of scholar," Miz Mandalay responded, rising from her seat, her clear, crisp voice ringing with the self-assurance and the apparent lucidity of her class (which was top-tone—her mother owned three States), "the Miz would be forced to admit that we have engaged in thirty minor counteractions and two major ones since the Succession. It is to our shame that we have proven to be as violent as were the Dongs when they ran things."

"Bah! Rocket Smoke! More violent!" cried Jaye Edgahoova, removing a spaceshoe and banging her rostrum top. She then grabbed from her satchel a copy of Plutarch's *Lives,* which she had been reading for the purpose of gleaning advice on warfare, and now she lifted it and brought it down on her rostrum-top with the explosive sound of a cherry bomb.

"We got to meet force wid force," she cried, falling back, as she sometimes did, especially when angered, on the rough, Jerseyish language of her youth. Out of common stock, she had fought her way to the top, tooth and nail, both feet forward.

"Dose Dames—" her aide took her by the sleeve and tugged. Her indiscretion noted, Miz Edgahoova renewed her attack with greater caution and better diction: "Those Yellow Mize were sneaking into our territory. If Miz Mandalay were as much of a Statesmiz as she is a scholar, she would know that our economy depends on the Tesla windmills of those Islands. What were we supposed to do—stand by and let them take them?"

"An extremely Dong-like argument" said Miz Mandalay, totally unaware of the bigotry in her statement.

"Oh no you don't," cried Jaye Edgahoova. "Just because you don't want to dirty your hands with jobs like that, and you let me make all the dirty decisions, don't mean you have a right to identify me with Dong-think. The Yellows was already shipping our oil away when my skyfleets creamed 'em."

"It could have been settled with reason," said Miz Mandalay with an unfortunate tinge of smugness.

"Reason!" Miz Edgahoova was boiling over. "Before we even opened fire the Yellows had shot down six ten-billion dollar Crawford Spikeheel rocketeers! Reason, she says!" Miz Edgahoova's aide tugged at her sleeve again. Miz Edgahoova pulled her arm free.

"I don't care," she shouted, pounding the rostrum top with her spaceshoe for emphasis, "I've said it before, and I'll say it right now, before this august body, those Yellows are tough titties. They'd have creamed us if I hadn't acted in time—or if you'd had your way."

At which several Yellow Mize scrambled to their feet and exited in a flurry, causing a general stir.

"Now you see what you've done!" cried Miz Mandalay. "You've offended the visiting representatives from the Mainland of Mizmou!"

"Bitches!" muttered Miz Edgahoova. "Them Yellow bitches!"

"Mize! Mize! Please! Order!" called Miz Mandalay. "Now then, it's time to hear the reports."

Miz Edgahoova, who had slumped back into her contour double-cheek cup, now jumped back to her feet. "I called for this emergency session," she cried, "and I'll call for the reports."

"Then please do," said Miz Mandalay. "Do let's get down to business and then some facts."

"If it's facts that this assembly wants, I've got 'em," claimed Miz Edgahoova. "As I was saying, them demonstrations must be stopped—"

"Facts, please, Miz Edgahoova," said Miz Mandalay coolly, "I called for facts."

"It's a fact that these demonstrations have been undermining the morale of the ruling Mize—that's a fact!"

"Speak for yourself; I was never more confident. These are great times to live in. Truly turbulent!"

Miz Edgahoova's rejoinder of "Balls," the filthiest of all words was spoken in such a low tone that none of the delegate Mize were sure they'd heard it. Still, it sent an electric thrill through the assembly. Miz Mandalay, fearing to reprimand Miz Edgahoova's language, also not certain of it, blushed to her tiny toes, but remained tight-lipped.

"The truth is," said Miz Edgahoova, "these are dangerous times. I repeat, the other day I told my class at the Female Bureau of Investigation that revolution *begins* in peaceful protest. As soon as the Dongs see that we are not willing to relinquish our power to them, they'll take active steps to steal it from us, just as the revolutionary libbies of the Succession did to them. That's politics! That's life! That's facts!"

"No speeches, please," interrupted Miz Mandalay. "No political theories—just facts."

"O.K., then I call as my first witness Miz Rabble-Mead, who has been working closely with me on this issue. As you all know, Miz Rabble-Mead is Ministmiz of Depopulation—also well known for her work in anthropological sperm confusion—"

Miz Edgahoova nodded, smiled graciously, and extended a hand for Miz Rabble-Mead. "Miz Rabble-Mead," she announced.

A pleasant-looking, rather tubby little Miz who had produced several Say-screen docus on the mating habits of the ancient Rednecks, tumbled to her feet, saying:

"Mind you, Gentlemize, I am a scientist, and therefore it behooves me to be Harvardly objective. I stand with the truth. Hem, hem! Now then. There is no doubt but that there is great unrest among the Dongs. I have here a list of complaints that has come into my commission's possession from the four corners of the Universe—which we are currently repairing—hem, hem! I have been asked by the Left Honorable Miz Edgahoova to read these complaints before this Assembly. I shall do so. But I wish it to be understood that I draw no conclusions.

"Number one . . . Three days ago, in the state of Femina, a large group of radical left-wing piece-marching Dongs paraded before the Mansion of Dr. Brothers-Marx—known to the Universe as Groucha of Femina, who owns said state—marched, I say, in full erection, and with marigolds jutting from the mouths of their erected members, carrying banners and placards bearing such legends as WE WANT A PIECE! and USE US, DON'T ABUSE US! This march was broken up by the Honorable Miz Edgahoova's Tactical Shrike Squads. Unfortunately, these wonderfully combative units were later accused by members of the radical media of having used more force than was necessary—of roughly pulling marigolds out and deliberately breaking off some few of the frozen members . . ."

"Get on to the next report," cried Jaye Edgahoova.

"Please go on," said Miz Mandalay.

"Well," went on the scientific Miz Rabble-Mead blithely, "Tactical Shrikes were accused of clubbing the erected members of the protesting Dongs; even of knocking the flowers from the muzzles of some of their members and trampling them—the flowers—underfoot with obvious glee—"

"Perhaps," said Miz Edgahoova, "they were a *little* too zealous. But they have a hard job. It's not easy to keep the Dongs down."

"This was just one incident reported in the past few days," Miz Rabble-Mead went on. "In Marthatown it was reported that small bands of Dongs gathered near the rotunda before a bronze statue of Edna St. Vincent Millay, whom the protesters felt had treated Dongs as mere sexual objects. They made reference to her sonnet, beginning: 'What lips my lips have kissed, and where and why;' which goes on to say that she had forgotten.

"The Dongs began by discarding their traditional dogsuit uniforms and shaving off their pubic hair. They then piled the pubic hair into a great heap at the foot of the statue of Miz Millay and set it afire while chanting—

> We've minds to use and more!
> We've been sexual objects too long!
> Our minds as well as our backs are strong!
> We're not ashamed, we're not ashamed,
> We're not ashamed anymore!
> The Dong, the Dong, the *Dong!*
> The Dong with the luminous nose!

Unfortunately, the Tactical Shrike Squad arrived on the scene too late to prevent any of this—"

"I tell you," cried Jaye Edgahoova, "we're flooded with requests—"

"Here's another," Miz Rabble-Mead went on, "from, of all places, Papal-Land. Perhaps this is the most significant of all. This report, though I hasten to add, *unconfirmed,* has it that in Papal-Land—certainly the *last* place . . . that the Dongs have been burning their jockstraps!"

"I think they look kinda cute that way," whispered a back-bench Ultra-blue to her colleague. "I like the way they bounce when they walk."

"Shhh!" shushed her associate, suppressing a giggle.

"—And using such cries," Miz Rabble-Mead hastened on, "as 'Dong Power,' 'Empower the Tower,' and 'A Piece of the Action'!"

"We've all grown quite used to such vulgarities," put in Miz Mandalay, trying to subdue the assemblage, which had grown loud and lusty. "Please go on."

"Well, here's another. Only yesterday, only a few blocks from this building, three young Dongs quietly infiltrated Mary Sorley's Old Tea House, and managed to get served."

An offended roar came from the Anglo-Irish Molly Maguires, the Lassies of Ire, contingent.

"I saw a piece," said an Ultra-blue Representative, "the other night on the Joanie Carson's Nightie Show, where they had Huley Heftem of the Playmiz Clubs—and they asked her what she thought of Dong-lib, and you know what she said?"

"What?"

"She said: 'We've got nothing against Dongs—as long as they don't take off their Donkey tails and sit down with the customers. She had brought a Donkey Dong with her who just sat there with a stupid smile on his face, and Huley ogled him and said, 'A Dong's place is in a heart-shaped bed.' It was so funny."

"Shhh!"

Miz Rabble-Mead went on: "—and these are only a minute number of serious offences. But, mind, I am trying to be subjective."

"Well, if Miz Rabble-Mead, as a scientist, finds that it's impossible to draw a conclusion, I, as a Statesmiz have an opposite duty," said Jaye Edgahoova. "The situation is dangerous to the tranquility of the State. I propose immediate forceful suppression of the Dongs. Come on, let's put 'em in their place!"

"Violence solves nothing," said Miz Mandalay. "Are you drunk?"

"Balls!"

"Miz Edgahoova!"

"*Balls*, I said—and balls I meant. Let my Tactical Shrike Squads loose on 'em. They'll scatter like sperm."

A little later, Miz Mandalay left the council, her faction quite sadly defeated. Miz

Edgahoova had proved once again what she had always known to be true: Reason has no chance in a competition with Energy. Jaye Edgahoova had won.

"Now," she said wrathfully, after the council room had nearly cleared, "when I get my mitts on the ringleader of those Dongs, that big dick Resurgius, I'll nail his balls to the wall. I'll teach him he can't steal my sexmiz."

Some few ears were cupped, but the brains attached remained mystified.

2

THE KIDNAPPING OF MIZ MANDALAY

"Miz Mandalay looks angry," said one of the Butcherbirds, the elite, degenderit Secret Service Shrikes whose duty it was to guard the Statesmize, as Miz Mandalay rocketed from the Assembly Room.

"We'd better be on our little toesies. When she's in a conniption tizzy she's hard to keep up with." Her two companions nodded knowingly.

"She's got her five-inch spikes on," said one of them, "they'll slow her down."

"I hope she doesn't go kissing through the crowd, spreading joy," said the other.

"No chance," said the one in charge, "she's pissed."

"Cripes, what an ass she's got!" said the second. "They rub against each other and keep coming up like an upside-down heart, if you look at it the right way."

"Yeah, and look at them anti-sex objects bounce," said the third, as Miz Mandalay flew by.

"Come on," said the one in charge, "we gotta keep up with her."

Miz Mandalay was already out the door.

When the Secret Service Shrikes hit the street, Miz Mandalay was wriggling into the back seat of her auto-chauffeured limousine, a pale pink Camille 3000.

Suddenly all bordello broke loose.

Three wobbly, crazy-looking superdupermodelmize, their makeup smeared, made a lunging hobble for the car.

"Hey, you there!" cried the Secret Service Shrike in charge. "What do you think you're doing?"

"Them are Dongs!" cried the second.

"Sure, look at those scrawny legs!" cried the third.

"No worse than yours!" cried another. "But modelmize don't have cods."

But before the Secret Service Shrikes could think what action to take, the three Dongs, who were dressed like high-fashion superdupermodelmize, had pulled Miz Mandalay from the love seat of her Camille 3000, and were now hustling the struggling Statesmiz into the wicker basket of a gigantic balloon, that looked for all the Universe like a golden condom.

"What's that on the top of the balloon?" asked the stunned second Secret Service Shrike.

"Tassels?" suggested the third, doubtfully.

"Feathers," said the Shrike in charge. "It's a French tickler."

"Cripes!" cried the second.

"Wow!" cried the third. "It looks like one of them ancient Quaint Wieners. I saw one in the museum of natural history."

"But it's golden," cried another. "Must be mustard all over it."

"Where are you taking me?" Miz Mandalay cried from the basket.

"To Resurgius," said the one with the bad hairy legs, the ugliest of the imitation superdupermodelmize. His green lipstick was smeared and he had at least ten o'clock shadow.

And up, up, and away, went the beautiful balloon. But at first the ride wasn't a smooth one. The glass canyons of the great state of Atalanta are deep and dark, and there is a long way to go before you get to the seductive sulphur of the sky.

Once the balloon caught in the towering marquee of the Porno Palace, and Miz Mandalay noted that "Little Men" was on the bill. She didn't have time to see what the second feature was, for the ugly Dong wearing the green lipstick had pushed them free. Up, up they soared, the sky above, the crowd below.

"Why don't they do something?" cried Miz Mandalay. By "they" she meant the three, now tiny, Secret Service Shrikes, who looked almost as if they were waving her good-bye.

Finally the great golden balloon cleared the tops of the skyscrapers and sailed out over the River Slime, buffeted occasionally by a sky full of commercial drones. Miz Mandalay could see the great LaMer Turnpike in the distance, and behind her even the brightest lights of the city were fading, and for all she knew she would never see them again. One crystal tear formed in each beautiful violet eye.

"What do you mean to do to me?" she asked the one in green lipstick.

"That's up to Resurgius."

"What's he like?"

"He's the greatest Dong in the whole Universe."

"How does he command such worship from his followers?" Miz Mandalay asked, trying to learn something of the Dong whose prisoner she had become.

"Why he gave us back our pride," said the Dong. "He showed us that Dong was beautiful." At which the other two Dongs in the basket burst enthusiastically into the chant—

We've minds to use and more—

But green lipstick quickly ordered them to shut up. "We'll have no more say until we arrive at our destination."

And so the roar of the passing drones was the only sound Miz Mandalay heard until the balloon began to descend far out over the LaMer Turnpike.

"Why that's the old Maidenform factory down there," cried Miz Mandalay. It still gave her a slight sensation of pride to see the remains of a Dong-supported industry in deflation.

The balloon settled, with a few bounces, to the roof.

"All out," ordered green lipstick, and Miz Mandalay climbed out of the basket.

"Where to?" she asked, rather anticipating her meeting with the great Dong leader, Resurgius.

"This way," she was told, and followed.

Green lipstick led her down a stairwell and into a huge, long loft-room at the far end of which sat a Dong, whom she assumed to be the mighty Resurgius, and none other than Miz Bet, whose month-ago disappearance had been the trigger of Jaye Edgahoova's wrath.

Resurgius and Miz Bet sat like two monarchs of old, side by side, each in a padded inverted cup of the ten-foot wide white plastic Maidenform bra that had once been a sign on the roof of the building. Around and before them, but with all eyes turned on Miz Mandalay, were at least twenty couples, Dongs and Cunnies, gathered like a court, whom Miz Mandalay rightly took to be Resurgius' top aides. It was humiliating for her to have to walk the long red carpet toward that perverted group of naturals. "He's trying to psyche me," she thought to herself, and walked handsomely forward. When she got close enough the court opened a path for her and she was brought directly before Resurgius and Miz Bet. To the latter, Miz Mandalay said:

"So, it's true then. You have gone over.

You have become a Cunnie. How disgraceful. A Miz of your rank!"

"Don't *Miz* me," said Miz Bet. "My name is Beth. You will use that name when addressing me, and when appropriate."

"Beth! What a name! It sounds positively Elizabethan," said Miz Mandalay, in a show of bravado. But she *was* a bit awed. "And I suppose this is the great Dong himself."

"This is Resurgius," said Beth. The Dong, a huge, bronzed, gold-and-flame-headed fellow remained silent, and this had the effect of making Miz Mandalay even more nervous and uncertain than before.

"Can't he talk?" she said. "After all, I am a Univacual leader, and have the right to expect respectful treatment."

But the flame-haired Dong's green eyes only glittered mischievously, if through his hornrims, darkly. Miz Mandalay turned her own eyes to Beth.

"Is this the kind of life you want?"

Beth was a busty, satin-skinned brunette with wonderful calves and long green eyes which Miz Mandalay guessed were only plastics, and which she now slid across her face to aim at what she saw as Resurgius' classic profile. Hypnotized by love, what she saw was an "R" chested super suit, made of red, white and blue plastic, red caped, and from which at the collar emerged Resurgius' stalk of a neck, and a head actually resembling Woody Allen's—an ancient movie star—wearing a pair of hornrimmed glasses.

"What do *you* think, baby?" Miz Bet said with a sexy smirk.

"How long have you been involved in this sort of thing?" said Miz Mandalay, ignoring Miz Bet's facial implications.

"Since the beginning," said Beth proudly. "Why do you think I ever had anything to do with that sow, Edgahoova? It was only in order to get my position in Dong Pop. I knew that from there I would be able to work under cover to stir the limp, demoralized Dongs to revolutionary erection. I first got the idea a few years ago. It occurred to me that if someone could induce a hardon in the Dongs, that would last for at least four hours, they could be a tremendous source of power.

"Then, a little later, one day at the office, I got the craves and sent out for a Dong. They sent Resurgius up to me and I liked his style, as who wouldn't! and so the next time I got the craves I asked that they send me the same Dong. Pretty soon, in the after-say and shared electronic vape, I came to see that he was the Dong that I was looking for to lead the coup. Brawn and brains! He and I together have planned everything—all those protests that had old Edgahoova in such a fit. She'd tell me everything, so I always knew how to counteract whatever action she might take. I used to laugh behind the old bag's back. But I *have* had my problems."

"Yes," said Resurgius, his voice like low drums, his speech like a tympanic tongue, "Beth means that she had had some difficulty convincing me of the wisdom of using actual force. Fundamentally, you see, I'm a pacifist, a lover—especially with my plastic Resurgius suit on—which has so many push-button valves."

"Yes," said Beth, "he had been rather overshamed at Shame-school, unfortunately, and I had a hard time of it convincing him that force must be met with force, as Jaye Edgahoova so well taught me. Look at those muscles!"

"Yes," said Resurgius, a little sadly, "the white feather in me has had to admit that force must be employed if we are to win our goal."

"Which is?" asked Miz Mandalay, sharp, little ears aperk.

"Well," said Resurgius, "my original goal was equality, but—"

"But," said Beth, "I have showed him that it is a fact of life among us simple simians, that there are oppressors and oppressed."

"And . . . if you don't want to be oppressed—" broke in Resurgius—

"—then you must oppress," Beth finished.

"And so, reluctantly, we have taken to the use of force," said Resurgius.

"This is very depressing," said Miz Mandalay, "and I'm your first victim."

"You are our very first victim," said Resurgius, "but you needn't remain one. You might consider joining us."

"Never!"

"Very well, but the invitation will remain open."

"And in the meantime," said Beth, "we should be able to get some great concessions from the Univacual Council for the promise of your return."

"Of course, you will never return me to them . . . ."

"Of course not."

"But if you were to join us," said Resurgius, "we naturally would still be able to get what we want. They need never know that you aren't being held forcibly."

"She doesn't *want* to join us, Resurgius, didn't you hear her?" There were sparks at Beth's temples, and her eyes blazed emerald.

"I just thought—"

"I'm beginning to see what you're thinking," snapped Beth.

"She's right," said Miz Mandalay staunchly, "I'll never join. You are all enemies of Atalanta Mizstate, and you'll soon come to a bloody end when Miz Edgahoova's Tactical Shrike-Police catch up with you." At which threat, Beth only sniffed as if smelling something unpleasant.

"You'll see," Miz Mandalay added rather weakly.

"She has spunk," said a Dong member of the Court, off to the left of Miz Mandalay.

"That's what gives her her leadership qualities," said his Cunnie. "But if she only knew what she was missing," she added coyly, looking up into her Dong's eyes, which were awkwardly crossed, looking down, back.

"What I'd like to know is," said Miz Mandalay, "why are you telling me all this? And also, I'd like to know what's in it for you, Miz Bet? You're from a good background and you had a top post. Are you, perish the thought, *in love* with this—this *Dong*? You can have all you want of him or a hundred like him, you know. Why on earth do you want to make yourself his slave?"

"She is *not* my slave," said Resurgius. "If anything, I am her slave. But there'll be no talk of slavery. Beth is my wife."

"Wife!" cried Miz Mandalay. "Have you no respect, to use such a filthy pre-Succession word? There is no such thing as a—what you said, don't you know that? It's against the law."

"Resurgius is the law here," said Beth, "and I am indeed his wife—wife, wife, wife!— and to me it is the most wonderful word in the world.

"As to your questions—we are telling you about ourselves because Resurgius, who is the kindest Dong in the Universe," with which she gave him a wifely side-wise smile, "hoped that you would see the light, and join us. I had no doubt that you would not. You are all reactionaries, even you, who claim to be such a liberal, when there's any question of losing power. For me, I had a father, a real one, not something from the sperm bank or the vulcanization chamber, and though I never knew him, I have had my dreams of what he was like. I picture him—"

"Never mind that," said Miz Mandalay. "Everybody at the top knows about your mother's indiscretion."

"I picture him," Beth went on, "with white hair, standing in the kitchen before an old-fashioned raystove, baking me an apple pie."

"Beth," Resurgius nudged her.

"Hem!" she cleared her voice. "Anyway, my sympathies have always been with the Dongs. There's an old song that my great-grandmother used to sing—"*I enjoy being a girl.*"

"Rotten old pre-Succession time," said Miz Mandalay.

"I know, but I love it," said Beth dreamily. "I'm an old-fashioned girl at heart, and they've pumped me so full of estrogen that I sag." She looked at Resurgius. "I swing and sway."

"And ambition," said Miz Mandalay, "the desire for ultimate power, couldn't have anything to do with it, I suppose."

"Naturally, I'd like to rule the Universe, be the Queen of all I survey. Wouldn't anybody? First level psychology explains that, how deep inside of us the only way we can feel truly safe is to be in control. You're just the same."

"Pooh!"

"Oh yes, it's true. You've got it in you, too."

"I suppose it's a throwback to your early disgrace. Very unfortunate. But do you suppose that this Dong is going to let *you* run things. He'll have all the power, *if* you succeed."

"And I'll have him, which is the same

thing as having the power. I can withhold sex and make him do my bidding. He is a Dong, after all. You love me, don't you, my dear Dong?"

"Deedy, I do, but much of what you two are saying is over my head. I'm just a simple guy."

"Sorry, darling. Now what do you propose we do with our guest?"

"Take her to the padding room and feed her. She's a bit too lean for my taste."

"Take her away," cried Beth, and then added, "and for Cripe's sake, get her a bra—the Howard Hughes Double Derrick."

3

MOONLIGHT SONATA

The Howard Hughes Double Derrick was a torture device designed by the pre-Succession Dong for the ancient movie star Jane Russell, whom the famous Dong engineer had apparently hated. It caused the anti-sex objects to be pressed upward toward the chin in an extremely uncomfortable fashion. Beth's insistence that Miz Mandalay wear that horrid instrument of torture, which had been found, moth-eaten and faded, but with wiring and padding intact, in a bin of specialty brassieres, was indicative of her distaste for their kidnap victim.

Try as he might, enemy that she was, Resurgius could not feel the same rancor toward Miz Mandalay that Miz Bet apparently felt.

Perhaps it was her beauty. To him, Miz Mandalay resembled a relentlessly blossoming female figure from a Frank Frazetta painting that he had seen in a secret collection of banished art. Much as he tried to contain himself, she steamed his hornrims and made him drool like a baby. After watching a few days of her suffering in the padding room, he relented in Beth's name and told Miz Mandalay that she might remove the Howard Hughes Double Derrick. To be sure that his orders were carried out, he stood and watched as she did so. The removal of the torture device prompted in him an even greater generosity of spirit, and he went on to tell Miz Mandalay that she might have the freedom of the top two floors of the five-storey factory, and also of the roof, but she was warned that escape was impossible.

The roof had an eight-foot-high chainlink fence around it, for in the pre-Succession days the factory workers had used it for games and exercise, and all the windows down below were heavily gated. The lower floors made dormitories for a crack battalion of Resurgius' troops and their warrior Cunnies, who marched with old-fashioned electric harpoons. The basement had been converted into a combined garage—one basement door ran out onto the slope of a hill—arsenal, and storage room for supplies.

Miz Mandalay decided to partake of the night air, and climbed to the roof. All the beautiful, dull bronze stars were out, for the month was Mae. Many lovely shades of smoke filled the air with the bracing scent of sulphur, and one could see the parti-colored signal lights on the half-moon's dark portion. It reminded her of the article she'd recently read in "Kosmo." *At the Meat Market in the Mall on the Moon, there are no cuts of dead animals, only meat, muscles and organs, developed from cells in a dish. Rumps, shanks, and livers that have never had a body. Vegetarians are in a state of consternation. Should such meat be condemned? But no animal died in its production. The meat is developed without nervous connection, so there has never been pain. There has never been life, in a sense, for none of this meat has had a head (sorry, brains are not manufactured). Should something be done? It is alive, in a sense, but its life must be a profound dimness, an almost nothingness. The Modern Meat Packers Association insists, on a Sartre-like nothingness. Skin, and fur, of course, are developed (grown) in the same manner. There are no animals, merely yards of skin and fur, fur of all kinds: mink, ermine, seal, sable. But you do not buy them at the Meat Market in the Mall on the Moon, you buy them at the Fur Coat Fair in the Mall on the Moon, where you can also purchase birdless feathers, and alligator shoes from alligator skin grown without legs or heads on huge trays in factories in Orlando and Boca Raton. Horns and tusks of all kinds can be bought, whole or powdered, at the Horn and Tusk Shop in the Mall on the Moon, and not one horn or tusk, whole or powdered, has had a concomitant animal: no elephant has been poached, no deer has been slaughtered for its antlers, no moose has been shot, no wild boar has been knifed, arrowed, or clubbed. But they are all represented at the Horn and Tusk Shop in the Mall on the Moon.*

Miz Mandalay hopelessly wished that she were at some resort on the Sea of Tranquility tonight, instead of being held a prisoner in an old, defunct brassiere factory. She wished she were eating an ancient Quaint Weiner, made of disgusting bad cholesterol, dripping fat, smeared with mustard and covered with sauerkraut, as people did happily once upon a time, at Coney Island, as she had seen pictures of in the ancient history books reproduced from the 2075 Giant Kloud, the Giant Kloud which was now so ancient and so full that nobody understood the early stuff that was in it; also a real Chesterfield cigarette and not a stupid humped Camel Vape. She was certain that nothing that came from the Meat Market in the Mall on the Moon could taste as good as a Quaint Weiner or a real smoke. Somewhere deep inside she was just an old-fashioned girl.

She wished now that at the last Economic Studies Conference she had voted for more funds for Poverty, so that this building and many others like it, that stood like ghosts of a bygone era about the fringes of Atalanta, might have been razed or perhaps converted for low income animal life or vegetable pod factories.

She couldn't help wondering why, for all their work, they had still been unable to get rid of poverty. Certainly her own mother had done her best to do just that in the State that she owned—Hollystate, which, unfortunately, was in danger of sinking in the sea, thus putting a final end to the film industry and its three remaining stars, who wouldn't leave—

the State that would someday be her own. Her mother, Miz Nansome, took as much money as she could from the middle-class Mize of her state and gave it to the starving tent people—O the grapes of wrath—and the Central State pursued the same policy under Governor Noisome. Somehow, it seemed that poverty just went hand in hand with progress. Well, that wasn't really her field of expertise, and she had no right to think of it. She cleared her head.

"Ah parti-colored moon in the most lovely, sulphurous heavens, you above all know that there is a tide in the affairs of Dongs, which, taken at the full, leads on to fortune. I have studied and prepared, and my time has come . . . ."

It was Resurgius! He stood alone, not twenty feet ahead, looking for all the Universe like an ancient statue of Eugen Sandow, pale, except for his glinting hornrims, against the night.

"Oh, shine on, shine on harvest moon up in the sky. I ain't had no lovin' since January, February, June or July—" He was singing.

"Ahem!" went Miz Mandalay, her natural good manners requiring that she make her presence known.

"Oh," said Resurgius, startled. "I—"

"You were talking to yourself, or singing, maybe." She walked up to him, thinking, "what a curious creature! I should like to know more about him! What shoulders! And what a small neck and what a big head. And what big glasses, and why the cape?"

"What are you then," asked Miz Mandalay, "a Say-screen that talks even if no one is present?"

"Yes," said Resurgius, turning to meet her, "it's a curious habit acquired early, when I had only myself for a friend."

"Then you had a Dong for a friend," said Miz Mandalay, wittily. "That's even more curious, don't you think?"

"You think so little of us, then?"

"Not so little, perhaps. But when I think of Dongs, I think of pre-Succession days. I think of the plight of Mize like my grandmother, and her mother, who led such lives of terrible hardship and virtual enslavement under the iron thumb of the Dongs."

"Your grandmother's husband, you mean, and her mother's husband. They, too, led hard lives, and solved their problems as they could. After your grandmother washed the stinky clothes in a washing machine, your grandfather took the laundry in a basket and hung it on a line with clothespins. They suffered too. Their thumbs were raw."

Miz Mandalay looked at the giant's poor little hands. "But see how things have changed since the Succession—"

"Yes, now Dongs are virtual slaves; I see that nothing has changed but the generations. Today there are masters and slaves just as always, and women are the masters."

"Well, I myself have fought in council to raise the position of the Dongs."

"Yes, you are a liberal, like my grandfather, Dr. Spank—"

"*He* was your fore-Dong?"

"Indeed he was. It was he, as you seem to be aware, who was the great Dong champion of Mize rights. I remember often how he would call himself a pig. If you will recall your history, you'll remember that it was he who was the pioneer of the Shame-schools."

"I do remember something about him in that line, but the main credit for the Shame-school principle is usually conceded to be that of Carrie Nation."

"I assure you that it was my mother's father's concept. He wanted the Universe to be a good place for his daughter to grow up in. He never disciplined her, and unfortunately she rebelled against his shapelessness and became a gartered Cunnie. She was one of the first after the Succession. She was rather wild, obviously. A great fan of that ancient actor,

John Wayne. In those days, if you'll remember, the Cunnies were known as Trampers. She was one of the first Trampers, wore skirts and everything. Of course, if it hadn't been for her slap-happy madness, I shouldn't be here today, and perhaps the Universe would not be on the brink of revolution."

"You really mean to pursue this revolt of the Dongs, then. . ."

"I have decided to do so."

"You'll never succeed, you know. You might have been able to deal with me, but you've made the wrong move by this kidnapping. Jaye Edgahoova will attack, tooth and nail, both feet forward."

"How can she attack when we have you for a hostage?"

"Bah! She'll let you kill me if you wish, then she'll have supreme power. Do you think my death would bother her in the least? It is only I that stand between her and total control. All you have done by kidnapping me is to give her the excuse she needed to annihilate you."

"Will she be so ruthless?"

"Absolutely."

"But why then did Beth, who knows Edgahoova so well, advise me to take this step?"

"I have been thinking about that myself, and I think I have the answer."

"Say, please."

"I doubt that you will believe me...."

"I repeat; say, please."

"You said that you at first believed in principles of pacifism."

"I did, until I saw that they were futile."

"Think, then, Resurgius, you are involved with a Miz possessed of a demon."

"She's not like that."

"Isn't she? I offer this possibility, dear Dong, for your consideration: Miz Bet—"

"Beth."

"All right, then, Beth is fully aware that this action which she has advised you to take will bring an attack by Jaye Edgahoova in its wake. She is staking everything on it. She is afraid that you'll fall back into pacifism if you have time to think of what bloodshed might be ahead. She is gambling that you will be forced into open war, that you'll be able to repulse Edgahoova's first onslaught—she probably still has spies in Edgahoova's employ who will tip her as to what that Miz will do, so that you will be prepared—and then, that you will reign supreme in the counterattack."

"If what you say is true, my Beth is treacherous."

"I doubt that her treachery will stop there, Resurgius."

"What do you mean?"

"I mean that, if you are successful—but you won't be—as soon as you assume control, you will find yourself chewing poisoned gum."

Resurgius stood, his large bronzed forehead furrowed in thought, lifting his hornrims from his eagle beak; then his forehead smoothed and his eyes sparkled with eked intelligence behind his hornrims.

"And earlier you warned her of me," he said. "It couldn't be that you are trying to divide and conquer, could it?"

"But of course I am," said Miz Mandalay, lightly. "Still, what I say is true. Eventually, one of you will turn against the other."

"I can see that you don't know what love is," said Resurgius.

"Love—between a Dong and a Miz—it's ludicrous."

"Love is never ludicrous."

"Not between equal Mize, but—"

"Ah, the liberal speaketh—

"I only meant—"

"Listen," said Resurgius, "let me tell you of my love. As a boy, like all boys, I was taught shame. I had to sit for three hours a day before the Say-screen while a Miz told me the errors of my toxic masculine nature. I was taught, just as my grandfather had conceived that the method should be, that I was swinish, brutish, insensitive, cruel, stupid, gross, with no capacity for fineness of sentiment or depth of emotion. I was told that even my organs felt as nothing compared with a woman's G-spot. In short, I was taught to hang my head and walk ashamed. I grew up during the period of severest suppression, right after the Great Succession. But one thing kept my spirit alive—a few lines of a poem that I remembered my mother reciting to me. They're by an early American poet named Robert Frost, and they certainly pertained to my grandfather, and therefore were a symbol to me. I don't remember exactly, but they went something like this:

I'm a liberal, you know what that is—
Liberals are people who never take their
Own side in a quarrel."

"Nonsense!"

"Perhaps, but that sustained me, kept the spark of faith in myself alive. It taught me to take my own side against that Say-screen at Shame-school. They saved me from my pacifist tendencies when I was taken to be a gladiator. I kept thinking of my opponent, but what good will it do to let him kill me? I have as much right to live as he. Or why do I not? And I could think of no reason. After all, it was *I* inside of me, someone with as much of a claim on life as he."

"That's the root of war."

"Yes, it is: circumstance and survival."

"Ugly."

"No, beautiful. Tragic but beautiful. Then I was taken from gladiatorial service, after sustaining a serious wound, and placed out to stud. As Beth told you, it was on a crave call that I met her. Which brings us back to love, for it was she who taught me the meaning of the word."

"Gratitude, not love, is the word for it."

"Well then, perhaps—have it as you will. But try to think what it meant to me when, instead of the usual treatment, she treated me like a person with a soul. Once, during the after-say, she read to me from a very ancient book called *Plutarch's Lives*, how a slave named Spartacus lead a revolt against his masters. She read how a snake coiled itself on his face as he lay asleep, and his wife, who was with him, and was a kind of prophetess, declared that it was a sign portending great and formidable power to him. I remember how the story stirred something in me, and excited me, and I fell asleep dreaming of it, and how suddenly the dream became so real that I could feel that snake upon my own face, and I jumped up to find that Beth had truly placed a small asp across my face that fell into my lap when I sat up, and, though I had been terrified, still I knew then that I had a destiny—for I had not been bitten—and that it was Beth who would help me to fulfill it. So you see, I knew that I loved her, and she me."

"You were grateful, Resurgius," said Miz Mandalay, genuinely touched by the story. "Perhaps we have been too hard on the Dongs," she added after a reflective moment. "But, you see, we have feared just such an enterprise as you now propose to undertake. It has always been my feeling that we should have given the Dongs the vote. It would have been a healthy channel wherein to release their frustrations and would have meant nothing, anyway."

"No," said Resurgius, "from your view, I believe that it was better that you didn't. A little freedom will always lead to the demand for more. My grandfather, Doctor Spank, made that mistake—giving the Mize that freedom—and I have paid for it with a life of slavery."

"Now you sound like Jaye Edgahoova—like a Conservative."

"A Conservative keeps what she's got for as long as she can, which certainly seems more like a natural impulse."

"You poor Dong, your mind, your soul, have been corrupted—"

"By society."

"By Beth."

"I've told you that I love her."

"Yes, you have, you poor Dong."

"But wait! As I looked at you in this beautiful sulphurous light, as I've listened to your commanding alto voice, something has come over me, possessed me. I want to sing:

>*Oh sweet and lovely*
>*Lady be good,*
>*Oh lady be good to me—*

"So," said Beth, stepping suddenly from the shadows behind them, "I had the craves and went looking for you, and couldn't find you anywhere. And here I find you on the roof conspiring, as it appears, with the enemy, and romancing her!"

"Oh, Beth my love, Miz Mandalay and I were just—"

"There are no Mize here," Beth interrupted vehemently, "she's just plain Mandy now."

"Mandy!" cried Miz Mandalay indignantly. "How dare you! You were nothing but a third rank official until that fool Edgahoova got a crush you. I have hundreds like you under me."

"Yes," said Beth, "but you're dancing to my music now, my fair Miz. And Mandy you'll be from this day forth. I've a mind to have you locked in the corset room and fed nothing but sliced plastic and radioactive milk. What have you been doing, filling this poor Dong's head with a lot of lies? What's she been saying, Resurgius?"

"Love . . . love . . ."

"Answer me, you big fool!"

"We have been talking about the lights on the moon—see how prettily they spell out the names of products. Look, look now; what does it say? One Calorie, is it?"

In spite of herself, Miz Mandalay wished she could cover a bit for Resurgius, protect him.

"What are you trying to do to my Dong? Turn his head?"

"You've done a pretty fair job of that yourself," Miz Mandalay rejoined. "You've got the poor creature thinking that he can become the super Dong of the universe. Don't you know you're riding him for a terrible fall? He's going to be deeply hurt when he sees that he's incompetent."

"Why, don't tell me you believe your own propaganda. He's got twice your mental capacity."

"Then it's you who should be careful."

"She has nothing to fear from me," said Resurgius.

"She's trying to turn us against each other," said Beth.

"How could I possibly do that?" rejoined Miz Mandalay. "A Dong and an Accidental should make a perfect pair."

"So, you'd throw that up at me, would you?"

Suddenly—perhaps it was Resurgius' hurt, green eyes—they looked green in this sulphurous air and behind the dancing light of his hornrims—that touched her, but Miz Mandalay felt ashamed.

"I'm sorry," she said, looking at Resurgius, whose eyes had teared-up. "Perhaps I shouldn't have said that."

"You certainly shouldn't have," said Beth. "Now you're going to spend the rest of your little visit in the corset room, and don't say I didn't warn you."

"Oh, Beth," said Resurgius, "I don't think we need—"

"Are you going to overrule me—in front of her?"

"No," said Resurgius, shrugging his massive bronze shoulders, and skulking off to a far corner of the roof. He detested scenes.

And so it came to pass that Miz Mandalay was thrown into the corset room, and was left to sleep on a stack of those revolting objects.

4

HER GOVERNMENT IN ACTION

When word was brought back in to the Emergency Session of the Univacual Council, that Miz Mandalay had been kidnapped by three Dongs dastardly disguised as superdupermodelmize, and that she had been taken away in a golden condom-like balloon, the members of the Council as a body fairly screeched for reprisals. This was very much to Jaye Edgahoova's taste, and she made good use of all this feline fury.

"Listen to me, Mize," she harangued, pebble-mouthed, "the Dongs have stolen from amongst us the flower of our regime, the magnificent Miz Mandalay, whom we all know and love. Who knows but that right now she is being tortured, or even deliberately impregnated"—oohs of hypocritical terror and horror from her auditors—"by the scoundrel Resurgius? First it was our adored Miz Bet. Now it's Miz Mandalay. Who will be next? Me? Thank Sappho for my whiskers. Something must be done!"

Here came a great tumult and shouting. There were cries for vengeance. All Dongs, no matter how innocent, should be rounded up and put into detention camps and the Ship of Dongs turned away.

"Great idea!" cried Jaye Edgahoova. "We must learn from history, while not letting it repeat itself. But—I must ask this question—might not such an action bring a reprisal in some form from the Dongs? Dare we to escalate, while they hold Miz Mandalay captive? But then again, dare we not? For what is the life of any one of us as opposed to the life of the Atalanta Mizstate? Sacrifices must be made in times of crisis. I know that if it were I who was being held, I should wish that the vote be for an immediate attack, that I might be made the proud and immortal martyr of freedom—but, do you agree?"

"Yea! Yea! Yea!" came the waves of mass approval. Vox populi! Vox dei! Long live liberty!

"Then let us withdraw, at this moment of crisis, my citimize, to contemplate the grave implications of our actions, and to make detailed plans of attack."

Volcanic eruptions of applause!

"It has been *your* decision," said Jaye Edgahoova, flushed with success, "I am merely your agent." She slammed her cup on the rostrum and withdrew, leaving the Council hall, and going directly to the Pink House.

As she trudged along with her squad of Secret Service Shrikes, she mulled over what she had learned from secret communication with Miz Bet; that Bet had no thought of making any concessions with the Dongs. Edgahoover could trust that dame. As she crossed the lawn, the usual gaggle of reporters from the various news services had spread blankets and were having a tea-party while waiting for a statement from Edgahoova's Press Secretary, Hedy Parsons (also renowned as a pianist and a heavyweight champion weightlifter).

Upon arrival at the Pink House, now a-bustle with activity, she called for her chief of Shrike-Police, one Furius, a red-haired exbarmiz from Hoboken, who was notorious for having bitten off the ears of twenty Dongs. Everyone knew that the story was true, for she kept the ears, in a marinated state, in a gallon pickle jar that stood on her desk in her offices at the Pinafore.

"Furius," said Edgahoova, "you are now looking at the absolute Boss of the Universe. The Dongs have played right into my hands. I can wage open war on them and get rid of Miz Mandalay at the same time. I'm thirsty. Get me a Pink Dongly. The kind with the big straws."

"I don't know," said Furius, pouring Edgahoova a drink, "it's too pat."

"What do you mean?" Edgahoova's pointed little red ears twitched.

"Well, why'd da Dongs make such a bad mistake?"

"I say dey was badly advised," said Edgahoova, lapsing into her natural speech.

"Yeah," said Furius, handing her boss the drink and shoving a skinny office Dong under her legs like a quivering ottoman, "but dat's what I mean. I smell a rat."

"If you mean Bet," said Edgahoova," I don't believe it."

"Yeah, cuz you got a case on her and won't look at da facts when you see 'em."

"You've always been jealous of her."

"O.K., but think about it. Resurgius never did nothin' like this before. This is her work."

"Of course it's her work, you fool. Don't you see that she's set the whole thing up for me. She's on my side."

"Dat's only what you *want* to believe. And if you win, she'll let you believe it. But if you lose, it'll be anudder story."

"She must know that I can't lose. Look at my armies—crawling on their stomachs for me!"

"You see, that's da point! Everybody, including Miz Bet and Resurgius, can look at your armies. But can you look at his? How do *you* know how many Dongs and Cunnies he has under his command? Look how widespread all these incidences have been. And I bet dat's just the tip of the iceboig. They might have spies to tell 'em where and how you'll attack, and they might have a network of millions, scattered through the Universe, to counterattack with. But still, I guess it's possible that they don't know all dongbots are out of commission, even ours, ever since the Univacual Council ruled in ancient days that they'd be immobilized in time of war. You know, Chief, dongbots have always been programmed for pacifism. There's nothing to worry about there."

"True. Course we don't know for sure how much Miz Bet knows or remembers of ancient history."

"She's a scholar, ain't she?"

"Balls! I still say they'd try to strike first."

"Listen, we know from experience dat Resurgius don't work dat way. You know what I tink? I tink Miz Bet wants you to attack, so she can force Resurgius into action."

"Balls!" cried Edgahoova. "I don't believe a word of it."

"You're blinded by love. You got a real superplough on dat witch."

"Shut up and rub my anti-sex objects," said Edgahoova, "I've gotta think."

Seven minutes later, Hedy Parsons called the reporters into the Situation Room for a press conference. Naturally, there was a fine turnout of press Mize—indeed, most of Atalanta's renowned journalists were present, and still brushing tea-cake crumbs from their chins.

There was Sandra Van Orchid, the five-million-bobbit-a-year representative of Public Say-screen and Frieda Unfriendly of Network C.A.T. Norma Postman, the rough-talking, curly-headed femfist, already-famed as a novelist, and now engaged in turning out such timely journalistic spectaculars as the recently best-selling *An Icecube on the Sun*, was very much present and already sputtering with caustic questions.

From the other side of the political spectrum came the two Wilhelminas; Sneller, of the arch-conservative Univacual Review, and Buckle, host of Public Say-screen's controversial Firing Squad show.

Jacqueline Anders, the Pink House muckraker was in the crowd, Jinny Restless of the Atalanta *Times*, and Petite Hannabelle, whose firebrand-liberal tabloid column, "Bubbles," had gained her tremendous recent popularity as a somewhat muffled roaring girl.

Oh, yes, they were all there, and they looked tense and exhausted from their long waiting for a scoop. As soon as they were seated, Press Secretary Hedy Parsons made the familiar, solemn statement, "Lady Mize, the Honorable Jaye Edgahoova," and they all got miserably back to their feet, as that formidable Miz strode in and up to the speaker's platform. She was the very picture of energy and decision. Anyone could see that the buck stopped with her (in fact she had several large accounts in Moon banks, and would surely be able to double her assets if the new missile deal went through). Having had little time to make up properly, she was wearing a stern face, with slightly smudged purple lipstick.

"Atalantans," she began immediately, "it is with heavy heart that I come before you this evening to announce a state of crisis in our nation.

"At five o'clock this afternoon, Mae 13, 3000, our Co-Efficient, Most High Miz Mandalay, was, as our best intelligence reports lead us to believe, the victim of a dastardly kidnapping plot, executed with precision and ruthlessness by a group of Dongs disguised as high-fashion superdupermodelmize, to the number of three, whom we believe to be under the leadership of one Resurgius, a former gladiator and call-stud, who has gone underground for the purpose of overthrowing our beloved Motherland.

"Our intelligence services have been working round the clock, for the past few hours, to discover the fate of our beloved leader; but as yet we have received no definite word as to her whereabouts. However, we are expecting word within the hour."

Jaye Edgahoova laid aside the sheet of paper from which she'd been reading, and leveled her little black ingot eyes on the journalists.

"Now there's the end of my prepared statement. I'd like to make a short off-the-cuff comment, however, in addition, before you Mize of the Press begin firing your questions. Off the Cuff—and let me make this perfectly clear—let me add that, though we seek no wider war, we are prepared to use all the vast power at our command to see that Miz Mandalay is returned safely to us and that those double-dealing pinko Dongs—and I hope they are listening—are brought within jabbing distance of the mailed fists of Miz Justice. We will show them no mercy, even if they should return Miz Mandalay unharmed, for they must be taught to ask, not what their country can do for them, but what they can do for their country!

"Now, Mize of the Press, proceed with your most explosive questions, please, and have no fear that I shall shrink from responsible reply. Miz Buckle?"

"I only wished to comment, Miz Edgahoova, that, to employ the oxy-moronic, and not as a mere epigrammatic device, but as an exemplification of my deepest feelings, your manifestation of the timocratical principle of cruel-kindness has caused me to become lachrymose eye for eye, drop for drop, pari-passu, and verbatim et litteratim, so that you have moved me into a state of expialidocious-supercalifragilation for the flag."

"Well, thanks, Miz Buckle—I guess.

How about you, Miz Restless? Got a toughy for me?"

"Well, Miz Edgahoova, you know perfectly well how I've always smugly opposed you—"

"Granted."

"But we can't let Atalanta go down the drain. Not until we've all milked her dry, anyway."

"Granted. I'm glad to see that we agree on something."

"And now I think that during this time of crisis we should all get behind you and support you. I, for one, promise to quit carping until after the crisis."

"Thanks. It took a big Miz to say that."

"I have a question."

"Yes, Norma."

"Well, to quote from that classic work by Ernesta Anyway, *Old Woman on the Ground*, 'Being brave is pressurized grace.'"

"Very true, but what is your question?"

"How'd you like to debate me? Or box?"

"I haven't got time right now, Norma."

"O.K., but have you ever heard of *In Praise of Silly* by Erasamiz?"

"No."

"Well, it's the latest best-seller, and I'm going to debate her, or maybe box her."

"Good, I'll tune in. How about you, Sandy?"

"I think we should get down to cases—the Public wants to know. Does this latest incident tie-up in any way with the disappearance last month of the Chairmiz in charge of Dong Pop, Miz Bet? And if so, how? All of us are familiar with the Pink House scuttlebutt that has it that Miz Bet defected. Would you comment on that?"

"Incisive questioning, Sandy. Yes, I'll be glad to comment on that, only to say this, in order to clear that up—so let me make this perfectly clear—Miz Bet—and let me address myself first to her character—is a Miz whose love of country is such that, there can be no doubt, whatsoever, as to the possibility that such an act, insofar as we understand it, but on the other hand, assuming that we have exhausted the possibilities of one, having employed every digit at its command, and on the third hand, all these for the furtherance of truth, as we know it, yet the iniquity of Mize were as easily viewed, in categoric terms, then we should most certainly reckon ourselves fortunate, and this State stable. I hope that answers your question, Sandy. I've tried to be specific."

"Thank you."

"Not at all. We certainly desire to have

a well-informed Public, for therein lies the strength of freedom and the free use of strength."

As Miz Edgahoova concluded this observation, she was handed a communiqué by Press Secretary Parsons. She paused to open the paper and read it, then she looked up.

"Gentlemize of the Press, I have just been handed a communiqué of great importance, and I am going to share its contents with you. Contact has been made with representatives of the Dongs, who have asked for certain concessions by our government in return for Miz Mandalay. They make the following demands—which I'll read verbatim.

1. A piece of the action.
2. Suffrage.
3. Right to hold public office.
4. Right to marry.
5. Dismantling of Shame-schools.
6. Impeachment of Jaye Edgahoova.
7. End the war on the dark side of the Moon and bring our girls home.
8. Don't buy any more of those spacejets from your brother-in-law—with our money.

"As you can see, these demands are outrageous and completely unacceptable, and leave us only one course of action. Happily, the Senate and the House of Representatives are on vacation; and, this being clearly a state of emergency, the buck stops with me. Therefore, this day, Mae 13, 3000, a day of infamy, I do declare open and atrocious war upon the Dongs. The little people of this country will fight to the last death-rattle—at home, in their beds, or on the john—and never will your government have owed so much to the acquiescence and asininity of so many. I thank you."

Furius had a nice double bourbon ready for her leader when the last reporter exited, and Edgahoova entered the little room adjacent the Ovary Office.

"Well," she asked, slamming the door behind her, "how'd it sound, Furius?"

"Chief, that was your finest hour."

"Thanks. How'd you like that part about even if they did return Miz Mandalay unharmed, we'd show them no mercy. That oughta get her throat cut, what?"

"Brilliant, Chief. And the way you fiddled Van Orchid's question about Miz Bet, if she'd brought a tape and played it back slow she couldn't get anything outa that mess."

"Your Chief is on her toes, Furius. Even if you're right about Bet defecting, it helps to keep the ball rolling that they think she was kidnapped too. Then again, if you're wrong about her, no harm's been done."

"Brilliant, Chief. But do you think it was

smart to declare war? Wouldn't a surprise attack have been better—a stab in the back?"

"It would have been better if those Dongs thought for a moment that we'd meet their insane demands, but they know perfectly well that the war has started already. They know this is a struggle to the death between me and Resurgius, feet first, tooth and nail. He knows I'm not going to give up everything I've worked for all these years—the suppression of the Dongs, the Great Succession, the fortune I'm making on munitions contracts, all the States I've been able to buy, and don't forget Pluto, which I own lock, stock, and barrel, and now I'm only one step from total control. Why it would be the same as giving up my life. Before I joined the Movement and became one of its leaders, I was nothing but a poor femfist living in a roach-infested room in Greenwich Village. I worked with my hands—look at them—gnarled and claw-like. I used to grow organic vegetables and peddle them on a cart through the Lower East Side. Sure, I'm a peasant. I'm proud of it."

"You should be, Chief. You're one of the great Deplorables."

"Well, you know what it's like, Furius. You've been there."

"And how! I got the Jersey ears to prove it."

"It's been a long hard struggle."

"But we've made it."

"Right, and ain't nobody goin' to take it away from us, unless it's over our dead bodies."

"Ya know, Chief, in a way, we're what made Atalanta great."

"A typical Atalanta success story, that's us. Gimme another shot, Furius."

"Coming up, Chief."

<u>5</u>

THE FUNDAMENTAL THINGS SURVIVE

At midnight came a soft knock on the door of the corset room, and then a key was turned in the lock. Miz Mandalay, who had been dozing off, woke with a heart-stopping start, and sat up straight as her curves would allow.

"Who's there?" she cried.

"Shhh! It's Resurgius. May I come in and talk with you?"

"I don't suppose I can stop you," said Miz Mandalay, pulling several corsets up to cover her bare knobs. It was quite hot in the little room, so she was sleeping au naturel.

"Of course you can—if you wish," replied Resurgius, through the crack of the door; "but I wish you wouldn't. I've brought you some news."

"Very well then, enter. What news do you bring?"

"Sad news, but inevitable, I'm afraid," said Resurgius, coming in and closing the door behind him. "May I sit next to you?"

"Come ahead."

Resurgius seated his plastic musclebound self on a stack of panty girdles and adjusted his cape and hornrims. "It is a sad day," he said, "but a day that had to come. Edgahoova has declared war."

"What did I tell you? My kidnapping, far from doing you any good, has only given Edgahoova the chance she was looking for, not that she wouldn't have made one up anyway. But now she can get rid of me into the bargain. My doom has come, I see."

"Oh no; don't think that. I'll see to it that you come to no harm."

"You? But why should you?"

"I like you."

"You like me? I—your enemy?"

"Alas, I do. You are curve-bound as I am muscle-bound. Besides, what good would it do now to harm you? I'll simply hold you until the hostilities end."

"You're a strange Dong, Resurgius. I should think that you would hate me and my kind for what we've done to you. You described your life to me earlier, and I did feel sympathy for you. Shame-school must have been a terrible experience for a young Dong of pride, like you. You know, I have been working to abolish Shame-school, or at least modify it down to modesty."

"You would have been a fool to have done so. It's always been the most valuable weapon that the Mize have had. Without it, Dongs would have asserted themselves long ago."

"That's what Edgahoova always said."

"Edgahoova's is a cruel, greedy, and warped personality, but she has a brilliant political mind. She has never allowed herself to become confused in her motives. She wants power. She was an Alinsky radical before the Succession, a leading revolutionary through it, and, once possessed of power, she became the extremist conservative in the Universe. That's how you get power and that's how you keep it. It's called triangulation."

"You make it sound like she never had

an ideal. I think when she started out she wanted to do good," said Miz Mandalay.

"Yes, that's how we all rationalize our compulsion to control."

"Are you like that?"

"Huuum. Probably, though I don't like to think so."

"Then why don't you desist?"

"Because we humans live in fear and search for power to control our little time while here. Death compels the search for power. It's natural not to."

"I would resist the compulsion to control, if I were in love."

"That's because you were born into everything on the up side. You'll find your true hunger in the descent," said Resurgius, shaking his head sadly.

"Pooh!"

"Kiss me."

"No."

"Why not?"

"No."

"Wouldn't you call in a Dong if you had the craves?"

"Yes . . ."

"Well?"

"But that's different. I don't know them."

"And do you know me?"

"Yes—a little."

"Not enough to say no. Don't you have the craves?"

"A little."

"Well then?"

"Well."

"There."

"Ooom!"

"Ah!"

"Oh!"

"Yi!"

"Mmm?"

"A-ha!"

"Wooo!"

"Weee!"

"Now then," said Resurgius, panting, afterward, "that wasn't so bad, was it?"

"Mmm!" purred Miz Mandalay. "You're a super Dong."

"Thanks, but I'd rather have you say you liked the real me, the skinny guy inside this parti-colored plastic muscle suit."

"Wasn't that the real you, Resurgius?"

"Shucks," said Resurgius, "you know what I mean. Say, do you believe in love at first see?"

"Absolutely not."

"Oh, I was afraid you'd say that."

"I thought you said you loved Miz Bet."

"Well, I do—or thought I did. I like her.

She has those wonder-curves ever since the operation, but yours are better. You know, I've been thinking about what you said on the roof—that I was confusing love, sex, and gratitude? Maybe there's something in that."

"And now I suppose you think that you're in love with me. Just like a Dong! Indecently romantic."

"But suppose I am?"

"It's nothing to me if you are. You're beginning to upset me, Resurgius. If you think that this little super frisk is going to turn me into one of your dumb Cunnies, you're mistaken. I'm a free Miz, with a life of my own. I don't do dishes or babies."

"Ah—but you're my prisoner—now. A prisoner of love!"

"Enough!" She waved him away. "This is what happens when one lets one's emotions get loose. I thank you for the excellent professional services that you've rendered me tonight. Now begone! I need my soma-coma."

"How hard and cold you grow!"

"How hard and hot you were! And how presumptuous you've become because of it! An inflatable plastic penis isn't everything—even when it's red, white, and blue. Please leave me, *Dong*!"

Resurgius went to the door; stopped and looked back at the raw hourglass lovely Miz

Mandalay, her gorgeous sands flowing upward in the moonlight from the window, her ultra violets not cold, but somehow hurt and angry, as if in an instant they might fill with molten tears.

"Goodnight, Sweetheart," he said softly. "I think I love you." And he was gone.

The tears flew from Miz Mandalay's eyes, like the hot sparks of a welder, while she sat and called herself a fool. What kind of fool she wasn't sure.

"What kind of fool am I?" she asked the night. A fool for love, answered a leaden star.

6

ANABASIS

The next morning, Tuesday, Mae 14, 3000, Resurgius woke to news that the Shrike-Troopers, with the assistance of the Tactical Shrike-Police, were arresting and placing into Detention Camps all Dongs who were so unfortunate as to not have gone into hiding.

The roundup was being shown on Say-screen, and to watch it angered him.

Beth, filling Resurgius' bowl for the third time with vitamin-rich Vegan CoCo-

Puffies, felt that the moment was propitious. "Strike now," she whispered into his crimson shell-like ear, "before they've arrested all those who would support you."

"You are right," said Resurgius, "this is no time for equivocation. The tide is at the flood. Let it lead on to fortune."

So saying, he contacted all his generals on a secret Me-pad channel; and ordering those whose headquarters were nearest the infamous Pinafore, headquarters for Furius and her Chiefs of Staff—three sisters named Claudia, Cossina, and Publia, who in pre-Succession days had been the singing group, French Kiss, and who now were suffering the pangs of the Change—to mount an offensive against that seat of war, hatred, and cattiness. Those of his generals whose headquarters were nearest the Detention Camps should set out to free the suffering, imprisoned Dongs. He himself would march on Martha, D.C.; his goal—take the Pink House and capture Jaye Edgahoova.

"But first, eat your Puffies," said Beth, and Resurgius took her hand affectionately and kissed it. She was always concerned to keep him erect and robust.

Within hours, Resurgius and a thousand of his cracked Yellow Berets were on the march, along the LaMer Turnpike.

Resurgius was exhilarated, now that he was in action, filled with the old gay combative spirit of his gladiatorial days on Sayscreen. Now all he desired was a chance to smite and smote the enemy. But he had one regret, that circumstances had prevented him from saying farewell to Miz Mandalay, that curvy-wurvy darling. He had never before held in the palm of his hand a behind so soft as hers, and, nobody, not even the rain, had such small hands (he had recently visited the underground museum at Patchen Place). The trouble was, Beth watched him like a hawk, and if he had gone to say goodbye to Miz Mandalay, Beth would have suspected his attraction. Besides, the little darling was probably sleeping late—after last night, he added mentally, with a slight touch of vanity.

He was thinking of such things as these when one of his officers who had been scouting ahead came jogging down the road, crying that a large force of Tactical Shrike-Police were charging down the tarmac to meet the Dongs. Even now, he was warned, they were halfway across Pankhurst Bridge, their lace collars like answers, blowing in the wind.

Knowing that this first engagement of the war would set the psychological standard for his Dongs, most of whom, because of their years at Shame-school, were a bit too hang-dong anyhow, he decided on an outrageous head-on attack, feet first, tooth and nail.

He calculated this way: his Yellow Berets outnumbered the force of Shrike-Police, and if he could make good time he could still meet those three formidable sisters, Claudia, Cosina, and Publia, while they were on the bridge. That way they could not range themselves against him with more than, say, twenty abosom. If he had, as he calculated, roughly twice their number, he could let rank after rank, of both his and theirs, hack each other to pieces, and with their last rank up, and then done for, he would still have half his army, and the way across Pankhurst Bridge, his first great obstacle, should have been cleared.

"Brilliant strategy," his officers concurred, and busily arranged the Yellow Berets into ranks of twenty. When this was done, Resurgius ordered his Moog player to sound the charge, "I'm in the Moog for a Billingsgate Rumpus!"

Onward, along the LaMer Turnpike, at double-time, ray-guns at high port, rockets to the left of them, rockets to the right of them, charged the six hundred. Resurgius led them, his bronzed pectoral muscles bouncing, his shapely calves knotting, his gold-and-flame hair like the beacon torch of the old Statue of

Liberty, his great hornrimmed specks bouncing on his nose, and his hearty cry of "Hi-ho, Dongs!" ringing back over the heads of the Yellow Berets like a call to mad inspiration.

The Battle of Pankhurst Bridge, the first engagement of the war that would become known to the historians of future centuries as The Battle of the Sexes, had begun.

All happened as Resurgius had calculated. The Yellow Berets caught the Tactical Shrike-Police when they were a little more than half way across the bridge, and those few survivors who were later to tell of their experience on that day, have oft been quoted as saying that the sound of the clash of the opposing forces could be likened to a bad recording of an old Hubert Humphrey speech being played backwards.

After raying down nearly thirty Shrikes, Resurgius' pistol was emptied of sunbeams, and, throwing it into the big open mouth of a particularly grizzly adversary, thus strangling her last hurrah, he drew his broadsword, and, wielding it so that it seemed to acquire the blurring speed of rotation of an old-fashioned helicopter, sliced his way to the opposite end of the bridge, and, coming from the rear, repeated this action. Up and down the files of Tactical Shrike-Police Resurgius went, like a white tornado, slicing them like liverwurst, making minced meat of multitudes, until the stagnant waters of the River Slime turned red beneath the bridge with the blood of the Tactical Shrike-Police. It was a complete rout.

The Victorias were done for. The Victors could camp and have a party.

When word of what had happened at Pankhurst Bridge reached Edgahoova, she summoned an Emergency meeting of Furius' Joint Chiefs and demanded an explanation of this disgraceful female failure.

"That force of Tactical Shrike-Police was caught napping, like sleeping beauties," said Edgahoova, her face aflame.

"You need a Pink Dongly, Chief?" asked Furius, concerned for her boss' health. "Or maybe a bit of distractive erotic zooaphilia; five minutes with Bob the Hog or maybe Sue the Sow?"

"Not now!" Edgahoova shouted back. "I'm too busy for craves! At a time like this Bob the Hog would just be boring."

Well, Chief," said Furius, "the Tactical Shrike-Police were just on a routine patrol. How could they know that Resurgius' Yellow Berets were on the LaMer Turnpike?"

"Balls! They know we're in a state of war, don't they? Now listen, I want no more such catastrophes! Aren't we all on Top

Bulletin Alert? Send Claudia with a large army to search out Resurgius and to destroy him! Break through that plastic suit of his and get to the little worm inside!"

"Will do, Chief!" said Furius enthusiastically. "Government is fun, just like the old Mafia."

"I'll take that Pink Dongly now," Edgahoova said, wiping her brow and breathing more easily.

"But, Chief," said the wounded and bandaged Claudia, ignoring Furius, who was mixing a Dongly for the Chief, "did you know that the Pinafore is under siege? How can I leave it now to go back out in the field again looking for Resurgius?"

"Balls! You just don't wanna leave that cushy office of yours and that cute aide-de-camp you've got. Put Cossina in charge of the Pinafore siege resistance. You're the ablest commander I've got. I need you in the field."

And thus it was decided that Claudia would take an army and go forward to seek out Resurgius and engage him in mortal combat.

The position of the main Dong army was vaguely known at this time to be somewhere in the squeeze-box area of the Pocono Mountains, and so Claudia led her army in that direction. It was hard to tell because nobody had paid the satellite bill and the satellites had all wobbled out of position, blurring human intelligence.

At eleven o'clock, Wednesday morning, Mae 15, 3000, Claudia's point-scout reported sighting the point-scout of Resurgius' Yellow Berets. He did not see her, she said. This was exactly the kind of situation that Claudia was hoping for. Her Shrikes, now refreshed with cocaine, greatly outnumbered Resurgius' Milltowned Dongs, and she also had the element of surprise working in her favor. Resurgius' troops were marching through a canyon of medium size, with steep escarpments to their right and left. They couldn't be more than twenty abreast. It was Pankhurst Bridge all over again, only this time the Shrike-Troopers had the advantages which Resurgius had had at the previous battle, those of number and surprise. Claudia was always ready to learn, even from a Dong. She decided that she would employ Resurgius' own tactic against him, and attack head on. She signaled her Moog player to sound the charge.

Unfortunately for Claudia's plan, however, Resurgius' point-scout, Tonto, had spotted Claudia's point, and returned to tell Resurgius that an army was moving against him.

Making lightning calculations, Resurgius

saw that he was in the same peril which the Tactical Shrike-Police had been in on Pankhurst Bridge, and reasoning that Claudia would charge, decided to avoid the encounter, which could only cause his army to suffer the same fate as that of the Tactical Shrike-Police.

Obviously, retreat was necessary. But retreat to where? He could never back his army up out of the canyon in time, with its sheer escarpments upward to either side. And he heard with deep concern the distant whine and cacophony of a Moog sounding the charge!

What to do?

Then he remembered the five backs of the Five Faces.

The Five Faces were stone portraits of five famous females which had been carved out of the gigantic rock-face of one of the major peaks of the Pocono Mountains by the famous Pip artist, Andrea Warlock. Not to be outdone by Mt. Rushmore's original monumentality, which had been made vague by winds and the sands of time, Warlock had one-upped the once famous stone chipper, Borglum.

About a quarter of a mile back, Resurgius had passed an area which might have been climbed without too much difficulty, and had asked one of his Dongs if he knew where it led. The Yellow Beret had answered that

that area had been made accessible by engineers so that Andrea Warlock and her aides could climb up to chip at the Five Faces.

"That area," said the Dong, "would be the tushes, as it were, of the famous females whose faces are there."

"I'd like to see them," said Resurgius, with a twinkle in his eye.

They face off in the opposite direction," the Dong continued, "toward the Pink House."

"What," said Resurgius, "their behinds?"

"No, their tits. You have to climb up quite some distance to get to them, but you couldn't see anything, because of the bosom extension, unless you were to lower yourself down the front on a rope."

"Is it a long way down—and out—if you go over their foreheads?" asked Resurgius.

"Oh yes, a thousand feet, at least," his Dong answered. Resurgius now calculated the risks. It was either a matter of climbing to the summit of the Five Faces, and perhaps being trapped, or of attempting a hopeless retreat down the backs and asses, out of the canyon. He daringly opted for the Five Faces, and gave the order.

Fortunately for Resurgius, before the Shrike-Troopers under Claudia had entered the canyon, Resurgius' Dongs were within sight of the hackles of the statues. True, they were trapped, cornered, with no apparent way out, except back down over the big asses, a thousand feet into the canyon, where Claudia's huge force could easily annihilate them; but on the other hand, they were still intact, and Claudia would not dare to attack uphill, which is to say up the backs of the great women of the monument.

Now Resurgius' greatest fear proved to be a likelihood. It was that Claudia, who was famous as a philistine, with an absolute detestation of art—and a personal grudge against Andrea Warlock, whom she had tried unsuccessfully to seduce at a Martha, D.C., political shindig—would call for a Rockcrusher missile to be brought to bear against his position.

Of course, he was right.

When Claudia entered the canyon, and saw what means Resurgius had used to make his escape, she did precisely that.

"We've got the Dongs trapped up there. They are impotent," she told her pretty aide-de-camp, whom she had decided to bring along, "call the Pinafore and tell my sister Cossina to sight in on the Five Faces with a Rockcrusher. While we're waiting for the fireworks we can have a picinicium."

But Resurgius had guessed as much, and even now behind his giant hornrims was bringing to bear all his powers of invention and analysis, to find a solution to his predicament.

He called for the Dong who had earlier told him about the statues and asked him:

"What, precisely, is their hair made of?"

"Well, as you might know," the Dong answered, "Andrea Warlock is a Pip artist, famed for doing the unusual."

"Just answer this one question," said Resurgius, "I'm not anymore interested in art, at this moment, than Claudia is."

"Yes, sir," said the Dong. "Well, the hair of the statues is made of kudzu vine, but in the case of Gloria Steinem, weeping willow, so that it actually grows, and has to be cut and re-coiffed every month or so. The State employs a large staff of gardener Mize who also are licensed beauticians to care for the upkeep. That's a particularly attractive *croquignole* wave that they've given Susan B. Anthony, don't you think?"

"Yeah, it's very attractive; but how long do you suppose it's been since they've had a trim?"

"Oh, I'd say they were about due."

"Then their hair is at its longest?"

"Mmm. Yes, I should say so."

"And how long would a hairdo like that, these *croquignole* waves, be if they were undone and combed down over old Susan B.

Anthony's face? Think they would they reach her knobs?"

"I should think they would reach down to her belly button."

"And if you had some of it cut and then attached to the end of that?"

"To her knees."

"And—"

"Yes, I see your point."

"Then get busy with those shears. We're going down."

Resurgius' plan was a brilliant piece of cosmetological invention under pressure, but it wouldn't have worked if it hadn't been for the fact that no one at the Pinafore wanted to go along with Claudia and blow the statues to hell. The O.K. finally came, but it came too late.

By the time Cossina, now back at the Pinafore, got the word to go ahead, that Edgahoova herself had overruled all who were opposed, Resurgius' Yellow Berets were already sliding and kicking their way down the noses of the five faces.

There they were—Susan B. Anthony, Margaret Sanger, Eleanor Roosevelt, Betty Freidan, and Gloria Steinem—with their kudzu and weeping willow streaming down over their faces, and Resurgius' Yellow Berets sliding down the strands right over their enormous titties. Resurgius was the first over a forehead. Dauntless, he slid down one of Betty Freidan's hairs, winking as he lowered himself past her left eye, and was the first to touch the ground.

Soon, all but one of the Yellow Berets were down. He had dutifully stayed behind in order to throw the ray guns down to his military comrades. Unfortunately, this lone brave trooper was killed in the blast that followed; he would later be honored at special ceremonies, at what was to become the tomb of the Unknown Dong.

Reaching the ground, Resurgius quickly regrouped his Yellow Berets, marched around the Pocono Mountains, and, entering the canyon by both mouths, surprised that picnicking and cavorting army of Claudia's, achieving his second victory of the Sex War, which was to be known as the Battle of the Five Faces. By the time the mountain was blown up, his troopers were already chasing many of the surviving and now unarmed Shrike-Troopers into the bushes. The success of the Yellow Berets in these sub-skirmishes must have been great, for many of the Shrike-Troopers, stout and nimble Mize, revolted over to the Dongs' side and became traitors, surrendering gaily to slobbering love. Resurgius returned their weapons to some of them, who joined the ranks of his best shocking troops, while others, of somewhat questionable sincerity, he allowed to become scouts, like the great Tonto.

Unfortunately, Claudia, who had been bathing in a nearby tributary of the River Slime, made her escape by running along the bed of that river with a twenty foot hollow reed in her mouth. She emerged, stark naked and covered with leeches, three miles from the scene of battle. However, Resurgius had succeeded in capturing her luggage, which consisted of five hundred assorted suitcases and hat boxes.

But, even though Claudia had temporarily made her escape, her fate was sealed.

Early Thursday morning, Mae 16, 3000, Resurgius' advance guard caught up with her at the Appomattox Public Baths, where she had retired in order to rid herself of the leeches. A few hours later, she handed her hollow reed to Resurgius and retired from the war in disgrace. Thus ended the public career of one great Soldress, who, alas, had made the mistake of calling down a Rockcrusher upon the images of five heroines of her own revolution. It is an ironic footnote to history, that today she is a quiet-living, unassuming grandmother, the wife of a village blacksmith.

Entre nous, Edgahoova was pleased at the idea of blowing up the Five Faces. More room one day for her big head.

7

KATABASIS

At this point in the war Resurgius began to experience his first difficulties with his own Dongs. They, alas, grown confident in their numbers, and erected with their successes, began to break away in small groups by night to go about ravaging the suburbs of Atalanta.

Thus was it ever, that achieved power from a common goal will immediately lead to division among the powerful. For, one of the ironies of human life is, to be anything, one must be oneself, and to be oneself one must assert against others, for the line between the self and others can only consist of such an assertion—the hacking warrior and the catatonic guru are employed in the same pursuit.

So now Edgahoova's position became visibly strengthened with outraged public opinion, and Resurgius, who had staked so much on the hope of making converts, found that much of the countryside had turned against him—disruption and war annoyed most people, for they had personal lives. And to add to his burdens, a group of his Dongs now suffered a severe defeat. To be sure, it was only a small group, and in no way representative of his main force, yet this first victory of the Shrike-Troopers had a demoralizing impact on the Dongs.

It seemed that Edgahoova, upon receiving word of Claudia's defeat and capitulation, had ordered Claudia's sister Cossina, who had sung bass, out into the field, and her first day out, with beginner's luck, she had fallen suddenly upon a party of Dongs, who through contempt and confidence had straggled away from the main body of Resurgius' troops, and so she had hacked these careless Dongs to chipped beef. It was an easy victory, for the Dongs were over-laden with portable Sayscreens which they had pillaged from the window of a local Amazon Mart. But, nonetheless, the victory had the effect of raising the morale of the Shrikes and lowering that of the Dongs.

However, this reversal was only temporary; for Resurgius, realizing that something must be done to recoup his loss, the major importance of which was moral, not military, counter-attacked, and, joining in battle, defeated Cossina's chief officers, and captured all of Cossina's own baggage—one thousand assorted suitcases, hatboxes and shoe racks—Cossina herself making a hairsbreadth escape.

When Edgahoova heard of this, she was fit to be tied, and in a quick double ceremony, though in absentia, she had both Claudia and Cossina drummed out of the army. No one claimed that this was jealousy. Upon getting word of her status, Cossina, enraged at having dishonor heaped upon her head by Edgahoova, defected to Resurgius, and was placed in charge of the army that was then laying siege to the Pinafore. With Publia now in charge at that venerable seat of infamy, the war had added to all its other ironies that of pitting sister against sister.

When Edgahoova saw the unpleasant turn things were taking, she decided to play her trump card, and put the ear-biting Furius herself in command of the most massive army ever assembled by Atalanta. It was not too difficult to put such an army together, for now a great many of the nobility—that is, those who owned one or more states—about sixty families—volunteered to help suppress the underdog Dongs, partly out of friendship for Edgahoova, whose cause of using the unlanded little people as a labor force to produce wealth on the land they owned, they were in complete sympathy with, and partly to gain honor.

There was anger among the Deplorables at being disrupted. In the streets they were given to singing openly rebellious songs, like "Curious Furius, She's a Dong," and carrying placards like the following:

The Vanderhorns own most of Arkanstate,
the Heebeejeebeezes own Kent;
a few score others own the rest of Freedom,
and we, the people, pay the rent.

Furius, a most canny warrior, instead of marching straight to the attack, as Claudia and Cossina had done, stayed with the main body of her army on the border of Martha, D.C., expecting that Resurgius would come that way, and sent her lieutenant, Mammius, with two legions of Tactical Shrike-Police, to wheel about and observe the enemy's motions, but upon no account to engage or skirmish. But

Mammius, upon the first opportunity, joined battle, and was routed, having a great many of her Shrikes slain, and a great many only saving their lives with the loss of their weapons. Furius rebuked Mammius severely, biting off one of her ears; and, arming the Shrikes once more, she made them give sureties for their new weapons, that they'd not part with them again; and five-hundred that were the beginners of the fight, she divided into fifty tens, and one of each, by lot, she bit the ears from, before the eyes of the whole army, assembled as spectators, to prove her power.

When she had thus sorely disciplined her Shrikes, she led them out against the enemy. But now, Resurgius, seeing that he would be overwhelmed, retreated up the River Slime, with Furius in hot pursuit. Indeed, by Friday morning, Mae 15, 3000, Furius had begun to overtake Resurgius.

And so, Resurgius made a serious gamble, and by completely avoiding the Pocono Mountains, turned his weary force in the direction of the nearest Spaceport.

Now during these trying times Spaceports were occupied by tremendous bands of Space-Pirates. They had complete operational control of most Spaceports, and a special branch of the government had been set up, by the year 2050, to pay them an official danegeld in order to assure safe and efficient space travel. These Air-Traffic-Controlling Pirates ran the Spaceports admirably, but they demanded complete freedom from government interference, and since they could in no wise be controlled or suppressed, without extended, expensive conflicts, government had found it expedient to grant them immunity and give them semi-official recognition. They became known as the A.S.P.s or Atalantan Space-Pirates, and their right of legal exemption from the laws of Atalanta was approved by a long succession of governments, proving once again, for the as yet unconvinced, that, in politics at least, might makes right.

In any case, these Space-Pirates and their Spaceports were untouchable, and no force of the government's would dare to march upon them, for, if they did, Space travel would be hopelessly snarled; and out of this had come the tradition of using Spaceports very much as churches had been used during the Dark Ages, as places of sanctuary. If the Space-Pirates were in sympathy with your cause, they might take you in—but they'd be much more likely to take you in if you could pay them some form of danegeld, like cigarettes (a valuable artifact), or any kind of booze or drugs. An added source of hope for Resurgius was the fact that these pirates had no one particular political affiliation, having seen clear through politics to its twin points of reference, money and power, and having decided to skip the bull shit rhetoric. They were comprised of all four sexes, and did little else but eat, drink, drug and fornicate in some amazing combos like drugged monkeys.

It was on the evening of Friday, Mae 17, 3000, that Resurgius and his weary Dongs entered the main gate of the Wanda Von Braunkirk Spacecenter and Port; and, surprisingly, to a hero's welcome. The Space-Pirates had been following the blazing course of the war on Say-screen; and, Edgahoova, recently having vetoed a bill to increase their tribute, for which they had spent a great deal of time and, worse, money, lobbying—having paid out a total of twenty-billion Bit Coins in bribes to officials—they had been on the verge of causing a total snarl in Space-traffic, when the war had broken out, and naturally were very sympathetic to Resurgius; of course, they also saw the possibility of a deal.

In one of the world's greatest backroom deals, Resurgius, too, saw this possibility. In fact, the deal would be his tribute.

After the formalities of the first meeting, the leaders retired to the control tower for a private session, leaving Resurgius' Dongs and the Shrike defectors to get acquainted with their counterparts among the Space-Pirates. Within minutes these had undertaken a marvelous bacchanal, so that for a thousand yards there was nothing to be seen but a hideously squirming daisy-chain, consisting of twenty thousand naked simian bodies.

Meanwhile, the leaders sat down before plates of assorted happy pills, including dream heaps of little red diablos, and began their private conference. The main spokesperson for the Space-Pirates was one Blackbeard, a Miz of robustious humor and keen mind.

"That was a most marvelous and unexpected welcome," Resurgius began, feeling her up and out.

"A show of unity with your cause, my dear Resurgius," said Blackbeard, popping down several little red diablos. "We Space-Pirates think very highly of you."

"And of my cause?"

"Which is?"

"Freedom, égalité, et fraternité—or if you would prefer, sororité."

"As a woman," said Blackbeard, "I see it as a fine and noble cause, but before you can achieve such high ideals you must seize power. Many heads must roll! There must be one of those brand-new electronic guillotines brought to the pubic square!"

"It's true," said Resurgius, "that only

through my accession to supreme power can the Universe hope to see again what you might call the just life. Alas, the burden of leadership weighs heavily upon my extremely broad shoulders."

"Take care, Resurgius, that it doesn't weigh down those plastic shoulders of yours."

"I suppose that you are making reference to the fact that I am in military retreat."

"You must admit," said Blackbeard, with her super red Revloned lips in a guileful smile that tilted her black beard slightly, "that it weakens your position. Immediately after the Battle of the Five Faces—incidentally, a brilliant piece of work—"

"Thanks."

"—we had begun to conceive of a plan whereby we might throw our considerable power in your direction, if—"

"Of course. I understand your position with regard to Martha, D.C., and Edgahoova."

"Yes, I knew that you'd understand. But now—here you are in full retreat. Things don't look very hopeful."

"You paint too black a picture, Blackbeard. Let's speak plainly. You are only trying to drive up your price for supporting me."

"Well, let's face it, Resurgius, the odds have altered, our gamble is a much greater one now. And let me remind you, that at this moment, we Space-Pirates are the only force standing between you and Furius."

"Yet you've seen that I'm resourceful, and might come up with a ploy that could alter everything again, and wind me into supreme power."

"Well, that is why we have welcomed you. We know that you've been in bad situations before and have survived to conquer. But still, we'd be taking a big gamble to support you. You desired that we should speak plainly. Very well, what is our support worth to you?"

"Fair question, Blackbeard. I propose to offer you, if I am successful, all the states now owned and operated by Edgahoova, to the number of three, with a labor population totaling three-hundred million. The revenues from those natural resources and industries alone should come to something in the neighborhood of twenty trillion ultra bobbits—the big green—every year, and all social services—schools, hospitals, etc.—are completely paid for out of the pockets of the working middle-class, who also support the poor through taxation, which will leave your revenue to be a clear profit, just as it is for Edgahoova now. What say you to that? Is that a deal or what?"

"What about a counter-proposal?"

"Go ahead."

"How about, in addition to those states owned by Edgahoova, throwing in those owned by Miz Mandalay, Furius, Cossina, Publia, Claudia and Miz Bet."

"Miz Bet only owns one state, through her mother, and I intend to keep that. After all, Miz Bet is my wife."

"What about the others?"

"Well, you must be able to see that I'll have to have some states to give to my Dongs, especially my generals, and, as for Cossina's states, I'll have to let her keep them, now that she's come over to my side, else what would she be fighting for?"

"Oh, I thought she was fighting for freedom."

"Don't be snide. Of course she's fighting for freedom. She's fighting for the freedom to keep her states. Haven't you heard of incentive?"

And thus they wrangled on all night and into the early hours of dawn, when the only sounds aside from the wind in the wires and their own voices, was the last soft sequence of random orgasms from the field, the sipping of rum, and the hissing of pot.

Finally, at ten o'clock Saturday morning, Mae 18, 3000, they came to an agreement. In return for her services, Blackbeard was to get the following:

1. All those states owned by Edgahoova and Furius.

2. All those Spaceports which were not now controlled by the Space-Pirates turned over to them.

3. Resurgius' government would double the danegeld now being paid to the Space-Pirates.

4. All Offense plants were to be handed over to Blackbeard's first cousin, who was a banker, and would make a respectable front.

5. Resurgius would guarantee the continuation of the war on the Dark Side of the Moon, so that there would be a place to drop bombs and explode missiles in order to supply a reason to keep the Offense plants operating.

6. Resurgius would, naturally, agree to a higher Offense budget.

For her part, Blackbeard was prepared to offer full cooperation with Resurgius, and to prove her good faith, they sealed their bargain with a kiss. Resurgius wiped his mouth with the back of his hand, and Blackbeard applied fresh lipstick. It was a distasteful end to difficult negotiations.

8

THE GREAT WALL OF FURIUS

Meanwhile, Furius had in no way been idle. Only a short league behind the tail of Resurgius' army as it had entered the gates of the Wanda Von Braunkirk Spacecenter and Port, Furius had her army set up camp while she contemplated the circumstances. To directly charge the Spacecenter was unthinkable. To summon down a Grandsmasher upon it was also totally out of the question, more especially in view of the sad fate of Claudia, who even now was pregnant with her first Accidental by the filthy village blacksmith with whom she had got drunk in order to console herself. In the midst of action she had forgotten to take her Defetus pills.

No, any attack was out of the question. If the Space-Pirates had taken Resurgius in, they would fight for him, and their numbers were large. Cripes, hadn't she warned Edgahoova of the folly of vetoing that big increase in their danegeld! Secretly she sometimes thought her Chief was a vain fool.

But then a plan began to hatch in her mind. And what a plan! If she could bring it off, not only would she have that Resurgius trapped and save the Atalantan way of life, to which purpose she was officially sworn, but she could make herself a nice little bit coin boodle on the side.

She got into communication with the Pinafore, the gist of her message being this (later made public as part of the Pinafore Papers):

"Have Resurgius and his Dongs trapped at the Wanda Von Braunkirk Spacecenter. Attack out of the question. Recommendation: Complete entrapment. Method: the construction of a moat, canalizing sludge from the River Slime, and the construction, within the perimeter of the moat, of a gigantic wall, to be known as the Great Wall of Furius, hereinafter.

"Naturally, the public would object to the use of Tactical Shrike-Police or Shrike-Troopers for the purpose, so I suggest that you give my aunt, Jennifer Thickneck, of Wonder Woman Constructions, sole contract for the work. Note: the following is to be classified Top Secret. It must be understood by Auntie Thickneck that I am to get fifty-percent of the profits paid her by the taxpayers for this work in return for the contract. If this plan is acceptable to all, a percentage of my fifty-percent will find its way back to all who approve. Naturally, my army will do the actual labor, as a service to the country."

Within minutes a bill had been passed by both Houses, whose members were reached at various resorts on The Sea of Tranquility; and, all agreeing on the matriotic importance of the work, the Shrike-Troopers were issued backhoes and began digging.

By Saturday morning, just as Resurgius and Blackbeard came to final terms, Furius laid the last plastic brick to the wall which would forever bear her name. This great and difficult work she perfected in a space of time short beyond all expectation, digging a ditch from the banks of the River Slime to the gates of the Wanda Von Braunkirk Spacecenter and on around the whole port. Within this roiling moat of sludge stood a gleaming wall of fine pink plastic bricks eighty feet high, with large ducts at its base to allow the River Slime in, and so drown those inside, and with Atalantan flags flying from every turret, which was twenty feet from its likeness to left and right.

Upon first sight of this great wall and the moat beyond it, Resurgius slighted and despised it as unimportant, but when he realized that provisions were short, he began to worry, as did Blackbeard, who was a Miz, as Resurgius had come to know, of hearty appetites. Soon there was great fear in the Spacecenter that they should all starve because of the wall; and it was that fear, and the hysteria that came in its wake, which led directly to what later historians have come to call The Day of Infamy, which was Sunday, Mae 19, 3000. At the same time, Resurgius, who was never neglectful of the need for military discipline, was drilling his Dongs in another part of the Spacecenter, and Blackbeard and her Space-Pirates, occupying all the available Rockettes, deserted him, taking off for the Moon.

9

ESCAPE FROM THE SPACEPORT

Just as Resurgius had discovered Blackbeard's infamous desertion of him, a great Spring deluge began to pelt the land and swell the River Slime, dilating its rather turgid water and sending it roaring with tremendous force over its bed of sludge. This in turn drove a great deal of water into the canal which Furius had dug, and, in a short time, caused the waters of the moat to rise perceptibly against the plastic brick of the Great Wall of Furius. And this fact gave Furius an idea that, giving the devil her due, must go down as one of the most brilliant military ploys in history; right beside the Trojan Horse, Custard's Last Stand, or the brilliant Ride of the Six Hundred.

"We'll drown 'em like rats!" she cried.

When asked by one of her lieutenants exactly what her meaning was, she elaborated:

"That's my plan," she said, "That's what the ducts are for. Get it?"

"The Spacecenter will fill up like a bathtub!"

"Right," said Furius, "and we can attach pumps to make sure that it does. As soon as Resurgius and his motley crew of Dongs, Cunnies, Hookers, and Shrike-Groupies see that they're going to be drowned, they'll make for the exit, where we can pick them off one by one as they come out. They'll have to leave before the water can get deep enough to do any lasting damage to the Spaceport, so nobody can ever blame me for destroying it, the way they blamed Claudia for destroying the Five Faces Univacual Monument, and I'll issue strict orders not to shoot any of the Space-Pirates, and that way we can avoid a Space snarl. How does it sound?" (It should be noted here that Furius was unaware of the escape of the Space-Pirates, for at the time of their departure she was in her mobile command post, exercising her hobby, pickling and jarring ears.)

"It sounds brilliant," said her lieutenant, "should I issue the orders?"

"Yes, and *vaya con Dios*, my darling. If my plan works, we'll have a victory celebration in the form of a Matronalia as soon as the weather clears, and I don't mean an old fashioned Matronalia, I mean a panting-mouth and erected-tongue Matronalia! Hot damn!"

"Oh, goodie!" cried the lieutenant. "I do just love a good Matronalia." And she jogged off to give the orders. Within hours the cry went up inside the Spaceport that the place was filling with water. Already now it was up to the average Dong's knees, and was rising rapidly.

"We'll all be drowned!" cried the more hysterical among the entrapped.

"Let's make a break for it out the front gates," cried the intrepid in unison.

"They'll mow us down as we come out," cried the timorous, "let's surrender instead."

It was at this point that Resurgius took action. Speaking in a firm stage-whisper over a loud speaker from the control tower, he gathered the attention of the disputants and forced them to apply reason to the crisis, saying:

"It is true that we have been deserted by our former ally, Blackbeard, and her Space-Pirates, and that we now must face the fact that we all may be drowned. It is also true that if we attempt to make our escape by wading or swimming out the main gate, which Furius has left to be the only exit in her diabolical wall, for there is no lock on it, and it opens outward, then we will all be killed; for surely she awaits without it, and she has vowed to take no prisoners"—this was not true, but Resurgius thought it might encourage his Dongs to consider a plan which he'd been hatching—"and isn't it plain to all of you that she wants us to leave by that gate, and that that is why she is flooding the Spaceport? If we go out that gate—either fighting or in surrender—we are done for. Now think on this:

"There are three elements which accommodate the traveller—land, air, and water. We cannot go by land, for there is an unscalable wall around us and an army in waiting outside its only exit. We cannot go by air, for our quondam allies, the Space-Pirates, have taken every craft that flies. Now, my ingenious Dongs, let me hear *you* solve the problem of your escape!"

From the knee-deep Dongs there arose a tremendous shout of "Water! We shall escape by water!"

"Exactly!"

"But how?" they cried.

In answer, Resurgius extended a bronzed and muscled arm and pointed at the administration building, across the way from him. It was a most huge, zebra-striped, plastic edifice which had been modeled on the classic lines of the Ancient Pan-Am Building, which had once stood, albeit a little drunkenly, right in the heart of Old Manhattan.

"Eureka!" he cried, his voice a dramatic and prophetic kettle-drum behind the incessant *Mama-poppa*! *Mama-poppa*! of the rain.

"There is your answer! 'Make thee an ark of gopherwood!' But we have no need for gopherwood, when we have a completely prefab plastic ark at our disposal. That thing'll float! All we have to do is to unmoor it, by which I mean throw all those computers out of it, and detach it from its foundations. It'll hold every last Dong of you. It'll be the Ark of the Deplorable Dongs! Get busy!"

Soon the Administration Building was afloat, and in a formal ceremony in the penthouse Resurgius was made an Admirable. "As surely as the water rises, we shall rise and sing," he had proclaimed, and sure enough they did. But it was a slow process, for it took billions of tons of water to fill the Spaceport and to float Resurgius' ark to the top of the wall. The new-fledged Admirable stood at his post in the penthouse all night as his fifty-story ship rose toward the stars rocking and swaying and creaking like an old tug at anchor.

Soon, though, the penthouse cleared the top of the wall, and Resurgius could look out over Furius' camp. Sure enough, a great body of troops was gathered at the gate, waiting for the Dongs to come out, and half drowning themselves in the waterfall deluge.

The whole countryside, as well, was under a greater siege than either Dong or Shrike could create: the siege of weather. In fact, Resurgius laughed to think, his troops were probably a lot dryer than those of Furius. Indeed, the whole countryside was melting into mud, and spattering back upon itself.

Perhaps it was this very feminine softness of the earth that reminded Resurgius of Miz Mandalay—or as he had come to think of her; Mandy—and of the softness of her behind. Oh, that he might be back at the brassiere factory right now, and have just a few moments in the corset room with her!

And as it so happened, Miz Mandalay was at that very moment thinking thoughts analogous to his.

She had been able to follow the whole course of the war on Say-screen; and, at first, when Resurgius had been winning, had felt the strangest mixed feelings of her life. She felt a definite sensation of fear that he might win, which no doubt would alter her whole mode of life, and yet at the same time she could not help feeling a certain pride in his success, as though, somehow, it were her own.

"It's the craziest thing," she thought, "he's beating me at my own game and I seem to like it that he is. What could it mean?" Then, later, when he began to suffer reverses, instead of being matriotically glad, as indeed it was her duty to be, she actually became terrified for him. She even began trying to think how she might be able to save him. "It's all very unmatriotic of me," she thought, "but I can't help how I feel about that big golden ape."

And now, just having seen the Nightie Show, and being aware of his being trapped within the walls of the Spaceport, and with all that water rising up above his silver boots—well, she just couldn't help herself, and had fallen onto a stack of corsets, where she was presently engaged in crying her eyes, and heart, out.

"Oh, my poor Dong!" she wept. "All you wanted was to be treated like a person, and look what we've done to you—turned you into a fugitive, a hunted animal, an heroic rat!

Oh, that you were only here in my arms, that I might comfort you! If you are fortunate enough to be saved, and to return to me, I'll never say those awful things I said to you again! And I'll love you love you love you," she added, panting.

And at that very moment the first floor of the Administrative Building rose even with the top of the Great Wall of Furius, and, turning and turning, like a rubber ducky caught in a maelstrom, it slid in the out gush of water over the wall and dropped, rocking, into the swirling moat, where it was immediately caught by the current and sent off at eighty miles an hour around the Spaceport.

Glancing up out of the window of her mobile command post, from her self-appointed task of sealing a jar of pickled ears, Furius saw the Administration Building go by on its first turn on the moat. Immediately, she went on Say-screen to report that victory was hers.

"Even now," she told the public, "debris from inside the Spaceport can be seen travelling at great velocity atop the whirling waters, and there can be no doubt that all rebels inside those walls have been drowned. Victory is ours!"

Upon hearing a late report of which, Miz Mandalay became inconsolable, and tried to hang herself by a garter. She had to be shoved into six corsets to restrain her powerful Amazonian self.

Beth, on the other hand, debated with herself whether it wasn't time to get in touch with Jaye Edgahoova and claim that she'd been kidnapped. In order to get away with that, however, she would have to see to it that Miz Mandalay's next suicide attempt was successful.

But Beth was too clever to leap before she'd looked. She decided to wait time out, and see if it wasn't possible that Resurgius had escaped. This wasn't to be attributed to loyalty on her part, but to an instinct for survival. For, if he were alive, Resurgius could incriminate her; and he would have to be taken care of before she could go back over to Edgahoova's side.

"It's all very sad," she thought. "I really loved that Dong. Really I did. And I really despise old Edgahoova. But I guess she'll just have to do. If Resurgius' army is drowned, what good is he?" But, fortunately for her, her respect for Resurgius' resourcefulness was so strong that she waited to hear some more definite confirmation of his death. And that would never come: for Resurgius, now an Admirable, was very much alive, and in command of the floating Ark.

All night Resurgius' Ark circled round the Spaceport and each time it got to the far side, where Furius could not see, fifty more of his Dongs leaped to the bank of the moat. By morning, he had regrouped his army on the other side of the Spaceport and was already drippingly on the march.

10

A MATRONALIA AND A MUTINY

    Monday, Mae 20, 3000. The weather had cleared and the bright gay sun had come out of hiding, dancing everywhere, over all, in its golden beam slippers.
    Furius, still believing Resurgius and all of his Dongs to have been drowned, gave her permission for the Matronalia to begin, and now it was in full swing. This Matronalia was nothing but a modern revision of the old pagan

rite, which had generally been held on the first of March in ancient times, and which consisted of the counterpart to the Saturnalia, or male festival, wherein masters feasted their slaves, and exchanged places with them, allowing them to give the orders, and generally bully and make fun of their masters—in other words, a day of Misrule. In the Matronalia of pagan times the same was done, the mistresses feasting their slaves as masters did theirs at Saturnalia. Now, in the days after the Great Succession the Matronalia had been revised, though in a somewhat different form, and to be held at any time the circumstances seemed appropriate—for instance, right after an election, or, as here, on the successful completion of a mission or task.

This revision of the old Matronalia was mainly the work of Sally Hurok, the great impresaria, who held the first Post-Succession Matronalia in Dolly Madison's Garden, to celebrate the success of the Succession. The Dongs, who were at that point completely enslaved (this was well before Abby Lincoln's Emancipation Proclamation of 1995) were allowed to mock and generally abuse the Mize present, who seemed to enjoy this turning of the tables immensely. Tootles and gay giggles rang out.

And so it was now, in Furius' camp.

The Dongs captured on the Martha Washington Bridge and other places, who were now prisoners of war, had been released from their cages for the occasion, and were busily employed in chasing giggling Shrike-Troopers. The Shrikes would run ahead, as in days of old, and the Dongs would run after them, stark naked, and holding their erected members in their hands, shouting such phrases as "Wait, my little chickadee," or, what many of the Shrike-Troopers preferred, "Stop, sexual object!" And then the Shrike-Troopers, also, of course, naked, would stop in their tracks, bend forward, and place their hands on their knees, and wait to be rammed. Such fun! Such gaiety! It made all forget the rigid ranking of the class system they lived under.

It was great sport, and everyone, including Furius, who had been rammed five times, was having a wonderful time. Furius had chosen as her partner for the Matronalia a particularly ugly old Dong who was toothless, but for a marvelously Dracula-like set of fangs, or dog-teeth, and was about to suggest to him that he might nibble on her ears, if he so desired, when a Highway Patrol Shrike came into camp, the bearer of bad tidings. It seemed that Resurgius and most of his army had survived, and were encamped not five miles distant!

If this was bad news for Furius, Resurgius himself had only a few minutes before he received equally bad news.

Only an hour earlier, two of Resurgius' more militant commanders, "Old Blood" Castratus and "Old Guts" Cunnilingus, had come blustering up to his command post, which was in a hollow tree, to complain that he had been misusing his army.

"We must attack," said Old Blood.

"Attack!" echoed Old Guts.

"But we can't attack," Resurgius objected. "They have us greatly outnumbered."

"We would have been in Martha, D.C., now, and eating slamburgs in the Pink House, if you hadn't started retreating. We think you're yellow! There!"

"Yellow!" echoed Old Guts.

"That's up to you two," said Resurgius, coolly, eying them through his hornrims, "you may think what you will of me, but I'll not have my whole army chopped to pieces because of your hotheadedness. Once my little army of Yellow Berets is lost, the revolution itself is lost. We are in a Dunquirkian situation."

"But we haven't fought a good battle since the Five Faces," cried Old Blood. "All we do is retreat, like a bunch of sissy scaredy-cats."

"Sissy scaredy-cats!" Old Guts emphasized.

"You know perfectly well that I'm no sissy," said Resurgius, flushing. "Look at these muscles," he added, flexing his enormous biceps. He cooly removed his spectacular hornrims. "And I am employing a time-honored tactic of military science, made famous by the great Roman General Fabius Maximus, when, in retreating, he caused his adversary, Hannibal, to overextend his lines of supply, and get way out in front of his skis."

"Bah!" cried Old Blood. "There's only one way to fight—that's attack, attack, attack! Rape! Pillage! Destroy! Blowup! Kill! Maim! Slaughter! Desecrate! Feet First, Tooth, and Nail! That's the only way to find peace in our time!"

"You have always disgusted me with your mixed metaphors," said Resurgius.

"Bah!" cried Old Guts. "Similes are better. Like, I like chaos and disorder. They're the fun of war." And the two generals stalked off cursing, hand in hand.

And, within the hour, Resurgius was brought news that Old Blood Castratus and Old Guts Cunnilingus had deserted camp, taking with them over a third of Resurgius' bravest Dongs.

"Well," he said, most philosophically,

"they're two of my best commanders; what good will it do to force them to stay? Perhaps they'll be able to harass Furius enough to allow me to make a getaway with my remaining Dongs. Still, I'd hate to see a third of my Dongs blown to bits." And so, he ordered that a scout go out after the mutineers and check as to their whereabouts, and see if they might need help.

It was just as Old Blood and Old Guts left camp with a third of Resurgius' army, that a Highway Patrol Shrike, on routine duty, happened to spot them. Thinking that she might get a promotion to a cushy desk job, where she could indulge herself in her hobbies of listening to high-decibel screeching electronic music, or slap-happy rap that rhymed really good dirty words, if she were to bring this off, she carefully followed Old Blood and Old Guts to Lake Gunk, a kind of cul-de-crap, which is fed by the River Slime, where they made a separate camp. She had to laugh, knowing the area, for Lake Gunk was out of season, and she knew that the mutineers would be mighty thirsty before long. For the fact was, that Lake Gunk was a fine place to camp, and the water very drinkable, in late summer, when the waste matter from a local Cathy Cola factory was poured into it—at which time a chemical analysis would show that it was about fifty percent pure Cathy Cola, which was a very strong germicide—but now, in mid-Mae, it became almost ninety percent pure Dizzy Detergent, and acquired the consistency of chocolate pudding, and was completely undrinkable and smelly—which was a good reason for finishing her investigation in a hurry, before nostrilitus set in, and they were forced to move on to find some kind of potable liquid.

So, this clever Highway Patrol Shrike, looking forward to the days at hand when she would be able to sit all day and listen to electronic noise, retraced her steps and, by following the trail from which Old Blood and Old Guts had emerged, came upon Resurgius' camp.

Hurrying back to the Furius encampment, she reported, breathlessly, "There's a group of apparent Dongzerters camped on the banks of Lake Gunk, and Resurgius and his main body of troops are just a bit farther on."

"Stunk? Skunk?"

"Gunk, Lake Gunk" repeated the Highway Patrol Shrike.

"You mean to tell me that they're alive?" cried Furius, tugging her left ear free of the fanged mouth of the venerable old Dong. "Are you trying to tell me that I failed to destroy them? That they got away?"

"I'm afraid it's true," said the Highway Patrol Shrike, importantly. She couldn't wait to get her reward. But she became a little uncertain when she saw that Furius was turning purple with rage.

"You!" cried Furius suddenly. "You dare to bring me such rotten news!" With which, she pounced upon the poor Highway Patrol Shrike and bit off both her ears, which effectively ended the latter's enjoyment of electronic music, and earrings.

Furius' first thought, right after pickling the Highway Patrol Shrike's ears, was that Resurgius might be planning to avoid contact with her army, so that he could make a straight run down to Martha, D.C., and seize the ottoman of power, in the Pink House. The more she thought about it, the more likely it seemed that he would do just that. Well, she thought, she could turn that to her own advantage. What she could do would be to let Resurgius avoid her and head south; then, using her Mephone, she would contact Publia at the Pinafore, and order her to place the Pinafore in somebody else's charge, and to bring an army up from Martha, D.C. That would put Resurgius between herself, in the North, and Publia, in the south; they would have him trapped. Post-hasty, she got in touch with Publia and explained her plan. Publia agreed, and placed the Pinafore, which was still under siege by Resurgius' Southern army, the Dixiecrat Dongs, in the charge of an underling, and started on the march north.

"I'm not going to attack Resurgius' main body," said Furius, explaining her strategy to a group of her commanders. "He's too slippery, and might get away. I'm going to wait until he makes his run for the South, which is what I'm certain he's going to do, and only when I have him trapped between Publia and us, will I attack. But I don't like the idea of letting those mutineer Dongs get clean away. Besides, I'm itching for a fight. And remember Fight makes Right. So I think I'll take a small contingent of Shrikes and go out to Lake Gunk and clean them up," she giggled, "or hose them down." She liked her own quip and, meaning to laugh, farted. "Any volunteers?"

Fifty Shrike-Troopers volunteered, and within the hour she came down upon the mutineer Dongs under the command of Old Blood Castratus and Old Guts Cunnilingus and began to chase them from the banks of the Gunk; but she could not pursue the slaughter because Resurgius came suddenly upon the scene and checked the fight. He had been told by the scout whom he had sent to follow Old Blood and Old Guts that they had also been followed by a Highway Patrol Shrike, and Resurgius had decided to go and check upon their safety—he arrived just in time, as historical fate would have it.

Now Furius was really furious. She returned to her camp, mustered her whole army, and set off to engage Resurgius, who by this time had left the mutineers' camp and returned to his own. He had tried once again to talk Old Blood and Old Guts into returning with him, but had failed. It was all very sad, for he saw his army, and with it his revolutionary hopes, falling apart with internal discord, like an upset stomach. Many of his Dongs felt blue and wanted only to make a run for their hideout at the brassiere factory; others, of a different temperament, inclined to agree with Old Blood and Old Guts; and, though not yet at the point where they were prepared to desert Resurgius and join the mutineers, they were bridling at the idea of retreat, and felt that attack, feet first, tooth and nail, was the only course. Resurgius' only thought was to hold as many of them together as he could, and get them to safety, so that, at some future date, they might make a comeback, a Risorgiopimento.

The fact that they had shed themselves of the small force under Furius, which had attacked them, had only served to confirm Old

Blood and Old Guts in the rightness of their stance. They forgot, almost instantly, that it had been Resurgius' counterattack which had saved them. Instead of leaving, they posted guards and held a victory celebration.

Meanwhile, Furius gave orders that six thousand Shrike-Troopers were to go ahead of her main body, circle round Old Blood and Old Guts' camp and, camouflaged as Birnam Wood, were to secure Small Hill on the far side of the mutineers' camp and wait for three blasts of her Moog, and then attack. First she would wipe out these mutineers, and then she'd go after Resurgius himself. She was already beginning to repent having sent for Publia, because she saw now that Resurgius had no intention of making for the Pink House, as she had thought, but was indeed, in complete retreat. It would be a shame if Publia, whom Furius now knew to be close by, should run into Resurgius and defeat him, and get all the credit, when she herself had done all the dirty work.

It was a minor misfortune of her plans, that her camouflaged Shrike-Troopers on Small Hill were spotted by two camp-following Cunnies of the mutineers, who had climbed the hill to pick raspberries and had begun to pull apart one of the Shrike-Troopers, who looked for all the Universe like a raspberry bush. Things might have gone badly for these camouflaged Shrike-Troopers, but luckily Furius at that moment sounded three blasts on her Moog and the full attack was on.

Within minutes, Furius was able to proclaim herself victor. It must be said, however, that of some ninety Dongs who were killed, only two were found to be wounded in their split infinitives, the rest having stood in their ranks and fought to the death like the fighting fools that they were, feet first, tooth and nail.

Old Blood Castratus was found, rigor mortis already setting in—it had been coming on for years—in a running position, face down, his old blood indicating a wound in the left cheek of his split infinitive.

Old Guts Cunnilingus was found in a similar position some yards away, but without a mark on him. An autopsy showed that he had swallowed a sunbeam up his arsehole, a lucky shot, even for an expert markswoman with a ray gun.

By the time that Resurgius got the sad news of the fate of the mutineers, he had already taken his remaining force deep into the Pocono Mountains, fully aware that he himself was being pursued. For the fact was that Typhus and Scrofula, two of Furius' more bloodthirsty lieutenants had been dispatched to go on ahead to Resurgius' camp and keep an eye on him. But, when Resurgius decamped and started into the Poconos, these two, seeing that his force was terribly diminished, decided that, instead of reporting his actions, they would themselves overtake and capture him. Unfortunately for them, they did succeed in overtaking him, for their Shrikes were fresh and his Dongs were tired; but instead of the defeat which they had fully expected to administer, Resurgius rallied, faced them, and utterly routed them, sending them in great disarray back to Furius, who bit off their ears for cowardice. It has always been difficult for generals and historians to explain the twists and turns of fate. The more intelligent among them have insisted that the explanations of historical events is best left to the narrative poets.

This strange success, however, turned out to be Resurgius' final ruination in the field, because it once again inspired his Dongs to fight. Now a large group of the more militant Dongs forcibly compelled their captain, one Erectus Custard, to lead them back upon the advancing army of Furius, which was exactly what the latter was eager for; the reason being that her Shrikes had begun to talk openly about the situation, saying that the honor of this war was reserved for she who would put some backbone into these slinky-spined troops and thus put an end to this war, which was costing everyone a pretty penny.

Furius, therefore, was eager to fight a decisive battle. So when, within an hour, she came upon Captain Erectus Custard and his Dongs, she was happy to supply him with the material for his last stand. (The Battle of Custard's Last Stand was fought in the late afternoon of Monday, Mae 20, 3000. Captain Erectus Custard and his complete compliment of Dongs were wiped out in this, the last important encounter of the Sex War.)

When Resurgius was brought word of Custard's Last Stand, his great green myopic eyes, magnified behind his hornrims, filled with tears. "The Establishment has proven too strong for us," he said, "and I, even in my Super-suit, have proven myself too weak to challenge it." He looked out on the draggled, mangled fifty-odd Dongs that he had left at his command and said, "Well, boys, let's call the whole thing off, shall we?"

They were too tired to answer.

For several days in his escape, Resurgius managed to keep just ahead of the advancing armies of Furius and Publia, which were vying with each other to strike the coup de grace.

On Thursday, Mae 23, 3000, Resurgius and his remaining Dongs came within view of the great spires of the LaMer Turnpike. There they disbanded, and, changing into the gray flannel business suits of Mize, two every hour, began to hitch rides from passing commuters into the city, where they took the long underground ride back to the LaMer Turnpike in surreptitious fashion, so that they might not be recognized as revolutionary Dongs, and in such circuitous manner returned to the Maidenform Brassiere Factory.

Resurgius, like a good captain, was the last to arrive.

"Well," said Beth, as he came up to her, shrinking inside his Super-suit, and on shaky, if powerful-looking plastic legs, and hoping for a word of kindness with which to soothe his wounds of the spirit, and shame.

"You've certainly made a real botch of it, haven't you?"

Debilitated, he slowly looked back at her. "Frankly, my dear, I don't give a damn," he said, turning his eyes away from her protuberant boobs.

Was this, then, the death of the Dongs?

11

THE ETERNAL TRIANGLE

"Maybe Dongs really *are* inferior," Beth went on, dressing Resurgius down. "I never really believed it, but I'm beginning to now. How could you let a fool like Furius chase you back here to me with your dong between your legs?"

"She scared me. There were too many of them, all hen-pecking me. I was bloody with bites. They reminded me of my family, whom

I couldn't stand—my aunts, my truly terrible mother," Resurgius said.

"We've all got families. That's no excuse."

"I had to retreat; I couldn't engage that many Shrike-Troopers; my Dongs would have been cut off."

"Better that they had, than to come back here so shamefully, and dressed as Mize at that. For Cripe's sake, take off that lipstick! It doesn't go with your five-o'clock shadow."

"We had to disguise ourselves," said Resurgius, wiping the Maxine Factor stain from his lips, "otherwise we would have been picked up and thrown into a Boys Town detention camp, because we ain't heavy."

"Oh, what a weakling!" Beth cried impatiently. "How could I have been such a fool as to bet on you—a skinny little twerp in a plastic muscle-suit! Say," she added apprehensively, "you weren't followed, were you?"

"For Cripe's sake, no," he said, "I'm sure I wasn't."

"Well, this looks like the end of my political career. I'm shit on a stick," Beth soliloquized.

"Well, what about me then?" he asked. "Don't you even have a kind word for me, after all I've been through? I did it all for you, you know."

"For *me*; that's a laugh!"

"You'd have been happy enough if I had won."

"But you didn't, you dumb Dong! You lost. Go on, get out of my sight, you loser, you musclebound piece of plastic, you skinny-necked intellectual brat! I've got some plans to make." At which, Beth's green eyes turned red with calculation, and Resurgius walked away, cursing his fate.

A few minutes later, he knocked on the door of the corset room.

"Who's there?" came the mellifluous, estrogen-loaded voice of Miz Mandalay.

"'Tis I, Resurgius, the great failure," said our hero in a sad voice.

The door flew open and the Amazonian Miz Mandalay stood looking down at him with big tears of joy and love squirting from her beautiful violet plastics.

"Oh, Resurgius!" she cried. "I had begun to think that you were lost in the Kloud and had become part of the babble of spacetime and I should never see you again." She threw her arms about his gigantic shoulders, and planted a dozen kisses all over his face, incidentally getting his lipstick on her cheek.

Resurgius was truly amazed by this Amazonian reception, though he wouldn't have been, had he been wiser in the ways of Mize, whose love is a process of incubation that, after months of stillness, bursts forth with a hearty cry.

"Oh, darling!" was that cry.

Slowly taking her arms from his shoulders, Resurgius stepped back dizzily and looked at her.

"I was seeking more of the consolation of philosophy than of physiotherapy," he said, "so I never expected anything like this. Am I mistaken, or . . . do you love me?"

"I love you, Resurgius!"

"But I am a defeated Dong. I have no future to offer you."

"All the more reason for me to feel as I do, for I thought you were dead, and that made me suffer, and I had never suffered before, and I found it a rather pleasurable business: and now, because you return, as you say, a defeated Dong, you need me in a way that could not have been had you returned triumphant. Oh, my poor, dumb, defeated Dong, how you stir me with your failure! How my heart did sing at the news of your every defeat!"

"And yet you say that you love me?"

"By sun and candlelight!"

"Would you—would you mind explaining a little? Not that I don't feel most highly gratified at the fact of your failed logic and increased love, but—"

"Of course, my poor, dearest Dong. But don't you see? No, of course you don't. A Miz understands these things. But it is only that, when you left, I thought you a worm; but it was possible that you might win, and return as a conqueror worm, to my dismay. We were enemies, officially, when you left. If you had returned a conqueror, it should have been I that you had conquered. But this way, with you defeated, I can imagine myself beginning a life with you; for I shall resign and we shall go to some satellite island and begin life anew as equals. Or I, a *little* superior, having come down in the world for your sake. And I will have you Resurgius, for you've tickled my fancy."

So saying, Miz Mandalay slightly giggled, blushed, and began once again to plant kisses on Resurgius' spectacled face. Soon she had pulled him into the corset room and down upon a stack of panty-girdles, where they exploded into action.

"Oh my dear Mandalay," he panted, "all the time I was away at war I could think of nothing but the incredible softness of your behind."

"And for my part," panted Mandalay in reply, "I could think of little else but the incredible plastic hardness of your codpiece. You are my sex object!"

"And you are mine!"

"And you are mine!"

"Enough!" cried Beth, whose demeanor had returned to that of Miz Bet, and who suddenly stood in the doorway which, in their haste, our lovers had neglected to close. She had been looking for Resurgius; for, once her temper had cooled, her knickers had heated up. But now were again thoroughly frozen.

"Look at him!" Beth cried in the dramatic third person. "Regard this weak and treacherous Dong in whom I have placed a Cunnie's hope! See how he uses me! Or should I say, uses my enemy! I placed my faith in him to give me power and he has failed! Still, my physical attraction for him has kept me as loyal as I know how to be, which I must admit isn't very loyal. But still! And now this knicker-knocking! If he thinks he's going to make a fool of me with another Cunnie, he's mistaken. He'll pay! He'll pay! I swear he will! This is it!" And she stalked off down the hall, her spiked heels clicking like hammers of revenge.

"She's pretty pissed," said Miz Mandalay. "You'd better go after her. She might do something we'll all regret."

"Oh, she'll chill out," said Resurgius.

"You mean calm down?"

"Yes. If she'd only been nicer to me this might not have happened."

"Yes it would, inevitably. Passion is hot—but sometimes cold, fire and ice."

Upon leaving Resurgius and Miz Mandalay, Beth went directly to her private office in the old zipper room, and set into motion a plan which she had had half formulated before Resurgius' return, and which seemed to fall into a complete form with her discovery of Resurgius' sexual betrayal. Not only had her plan to seize supreme power been wrecked by Resurgius' military ineptitudes, as she saw them, but her sexual pride had been injured, and revenge was uppermost in her mind. Thus it was that, in a fit of blind rage, she tapped out the following message to Edgahoova, using her personal, Me-phone:

Dear Jaye:

You are so right. Dongs are monsters at heart. It's true—in case you might have heard it—that my heart betrayed me, and I almost fell for Resurgius with a real plough—but not like the superplough that I've always had on you, dear Jaye.

You must believe me when I tell you that when I dropped out of sight nearly six weeks ago, I did it for you. You see, Jaye, I had a plan, and I knew that you wouldn't O.K. it, because it would put me in great danger, and you wouldn't want your special curvy Cunnie-wunnie in danger, I know.

I had met this Resurgius when he came to me on a crave call, when he was a stud. I discovered that he was the leader of a plot to overthrow the government. It was then that I decided to sacrifice myself, if need be, to save you and our blessed ovarian government from overthrow.

Naturally, I could trust no one, for he has spies everywhere. So I took it upon myself to pretend to befriend him, fall in love, and run off with him. You see, I was playing a dangerous game and taking great risks for our Motherland.

Well, he has a strong mind, powerful persuasiveness, and large muscles, and it wasn't long before I found myself in his power—under his spell, I might almost put it. He is such a force for evil, as you must know.

But my head has cleared! Won't you take your little Cunnie-wunnie back into your giant lioness heart? You know that it has always been you for me. I've made a great fool of myself. But I'm still your little playmate. Remember?

And now I'm ready to complete the job that I set out to do. Here's my plan: If you'll welcome me back into your good graces, I'll tell you where Resurgius is hiding.

Only—naturally, I have to take some care to my future—I require that you reply to this proposition on Public Say-screen, and that you make a public declaration about me, the gist of which should be: that you have word that I'm safe, and am soon to be released back to my duties by the rebel Dongs. Also, that you have confirmed that I am innocent of any wrong-doing, as indeed I am, unless it is a crime to be hypnotized and misused, and abused. Upon seeing this on Say-screen, you will within minutes receive word from me of Resurgius' whereabouts.

Hanging my hopes upon this thin thread, as well as upon the steel girder which I know your love to be, once given, and looking forward to our loving reunion, I am, as always,

Your Miz Bet

"It isn't much," Beth thought, pushing the activation button of the direct-line writer, "but it's all I've got. If horrid old Edgahoova's still as crazy about me as she was, she'll go for it. I might have my old job back by tomorrow. Oh, but Ugh! How I hate the thought of having her big paws on me again, pushing my head into her hairy bosom. I feel so different since the operation, kind of pro-fem. Eeek!"

Indeed, these thoughts greatly depleted her hope of re-establishment.

She turned on the Say-screen in time to catch the last of her favorite soap opera, *The Killing of Brother Georgette*. While she waited for reply, she sang sadly to herself:

He was my Dong
But he done me wrong . . .

At this very moment, Edgahoova was discussing Miz Bet's message with Furius who, fresh from battle, was soaking in a marble tub, a Pink Dongly with a banned plastic straw, resting on its wide edge.

"This ought to convince you if nothing else has," said Furius. "Can't you see through that transparent piece of ass? Can't you read between the lines?"

"I'm not exactly stupid, Furius," said Edgahoova. "I didn't work my way up to the top of the heap, Queen of the Mountain, Mistress Miz of the Pink House, by being dumb, you know. I've got plenty of animal cunning, if not brains, plus a law degree from Harvest. I'm a politician."

"Sure you have, Chief, you're from Newark, originally, aincha? Down Neck? I never thought different. But where that Miz Bet is concerned—well—"

"O.K.," said Edgahoova, "I've still got a crush on Miz Bet, but I can read too. But that's up to me. I'll decide what to do with Miz Bet later. But right now, let me give you a good example of the cunning that has made me great."

"Fire away, Chief," said Furius, sponging her muscular arms.

"Well, it's clear that Miz Bet is now disposed to do as I order, regardless of whatever else she's done to date, right?"

"Right! No doubt about that part of it. She's scared now, and has obviously turned against Resurgius."

"O.K. So let's extract a high fee for our good will, false though it may—and I say *may*—be. I've got to see her before I make up my mind about that."

"But what's the fee, Chief?"

"Well, if she tips us as to where that Resurgius is hiding, and we get there and clean the place out, we're going to find Miz Mandalay. Now I don't want that liberal dame in my hair ever again. I want complete control of Atalanta. Ain't that what we all lust for? Actually, I'd like to have her bumped, one way or the other. But there's bound to be too much public notice on Resurgius' capture. It's a touchy situation. Something might go wrong if we bumped her then and there, and later it'd be even harder to get away with."

"You got a point, all right," said Furius.

"But how're we gonna get rid of her?"

"That'll be the price we ask of Miz Bet—the price of that clean slate she wants."

"Say, Chief, that's a great piece of cunning. How'll we work it?"

"You'll see. Miz Bet's an experienced diplomat. She'll get the message."

And, suddenly, Click! There it was: The Message!

Beth leaned forward in anticipation. An announcement had just been made that Jaye Edgahoova was to speak next. And there she was now, on Say-screen, Jaye Edgahoova herself.

"My gentle Mize," she began. "I have requested Say-screen time for the purpose of bringing you up to date on the conditions prevailing in Atalanta during this time of Dong erection.

"As you may know, our great and good military leaders, the great Publia and the immortal Furius, have today completely routed the Dong army which has threatened our happy way of life, and which was commanded by the infamous Dong, Resurgius. A Dong-count reveals that many millions of Dongs were killed, whereas our fine Shrike-Troopers suffered no more losses than a few red tips from their longer fingernails. Of course, these things must be expected. Sacrifice is a part of war. It is the price you pay for our feminine freedom. As Abby Lincoln once said, 'Better dead than left ignored.' And in the words of the immortal Wilma Shakehips, author of 'Omelet' and 'Queen Leer,' 'The poor are sad because they are good. Therefore, take heart!' Ah, yes, inspiring words from the Immortal Bardess of Avon Calling. Let us heed them!

"Yes, the broken fingernails will grow back in a new burst of freedom. And when they do, we shall paint them in the colors of Atalanta's flag—feet first, tooth and nail! Now then, let's get down to cases.

"It is an unfortunate fact that Resurgius himself escaped capture, but it appears, even so, that he has come to the end of his ugly, male-factions.

"Allow me to elaborate. No doubt many of you have wondered about the strange disappearance of Miz Bet, one of my top aides. The fact is, six weeks ago I sent Miz Bet on a most hazardous mission. Her purpose: to infiltrate Resurgius' secret headquarters. And now my foresight and planning has borne fruit.

"I have, only a short time ago, received information as to the current state of affairs in Resurgius' hideaway.

"It is tragic news.

"Our reports indicate that Resurgius, the

infamous Dong leader, and the charismatic Miz Mandalay, whom you all know, and who it now appears was the victim only of a staged—I repeat, *staged*—kidnapping, and is in fact a spy and a traitor, and has been, in fact, Resurgius' accomplice and consort, have died in an evil suicide pact, directly resulting from Resurgius' defeat.

"It troubles me not a little to be forced to report that Miz Mandalay, formerly a leading member of the Univacual Council, has died in dishonor. But she died before she could do any more harm, and perhaps that's as well. Guten Abend, and as we Atalantans always say when toasting a cheerie great event—not Cheers, not Prosit, but Up Yours!"

"So," said Beth to herself, turning off the Say-screen, "that's what the old devil asks of me, is it? Well, that seems like a pretty fair deal to me. She did clear me, pretty much, and that's a good sign. And he was my Dong, and he did do me wrong. And I hate that super bitch Mandalay anyway. But she died before she could do any more harm, Edgahoova said. That means I'd better work fast. Let's see, how shall I do it?"

Just then Resurgius' top remaining Dong Commander came jogging up the hall on powerful thighs and blistered feet, and pounded on the door. She pulled it open.

"I'm looking for Resurgius," he said.

"Is it about that Edgahoova speech that was on just now?"

"Yeah."

"Don't tell me you fell for that," said Beth. "You Dongs will believe anything."

"What do you mean?"

"That's exactly what Edgahoova's trying to do. She's trying to turn us against each other. You let me handle this. I'll tell Resurgius about it when he wakes up; he's sound asleep, poor Dong, exhausted from the war. You go back now and tell everybody to calm down."

"But—"

"Do as I say, unless you want me to report you to Resurgius."

"Well—"

"Go on, now. Everything'll be ultra."

Looking unsure, the Dong turned and trotted back on powerful thighs and tender feet in the direction from which he'd come, which was Nowheresville.

"I have to act fast," thought Beth. "I know. I've got it. With a Spartacus snake I made him a leader, and with a Spartacus snake I'll poison him."

Beth ran to the kitchen—she was an excellent cook—rustled up two plates of green spaghetti with clam sauce, placed a little green asp in each plate, covered it, and took it into the hall, where she saw a passing Dong, and, giving him the tray, told him to take it to Resurgius in the corset room and asp no questions.

*He was my Dong
But he done me wrong . . .*

she sang, walking away, and dreaming of reinstatement.

"Say, that looks good," said Resurgius, taking the tray from the Dong, "It's my favorite, green spaghetti and clam sauce. Wow, I sure did work up an appetite!"

"Me too," purred Miz Mandalay. "I'm starved."

Fortunately for them both, Resurgius, who had never mastered the art of Italian eating (by which we mean the use of spoon and fork and the winding up of spaghetti), and had been in the habit of feeding himself spaghetti with his fingers, as babies eat Gerber food, reached into his dish and, by chance, pulled an asp out by its tail.

"What's this?" he said. "This spaghetti squirms about as if it were alive. Perhaps it hasn't been cooked enough."

"I should say not," said Miz Mandalay, who had never been into a kitchen in her life.

"Why they haven't even cut its head off. See, its tiny eyes are blinking."

"Nonsense," said Resurgius. "Spaghetti doesn't have eyes. It's made of whole food paste."

"It does so have eyes," said Miz Mandalay, "and a little forked tongue too, judging by the one you're holding."

Resurgius raised the thing up higher to see. He focused his hornrims.

"Cripes!" he cried. "That's not green spaghetti, that's a snake!"

Letting go of the tail-end of the little asp, he knocked Mandalay's plate from her hand, and dumped his own, and began stomping all over the squirming green stuff. Fortunately, he had not removed his hobnail boots while making love (he needed traction)—this was not inconsideration on his part; Mandalay simply hadn't given him the chance—and now the hobnail bottoms went to work chopping up snakes and spaghetti alike.

"I don't know which is which," he cried, in slight hysteria, "but I'll kill all of it. This dish'll be fit to eat before I'm done."

And indeed, he made a mincemeat of the whole mess. When he was done he flopped down next to Miz Mandalay on a stack of corsets, his giant plastic pectorals heaving.

"This could only be the work of one person," said Mandalay.

"Beth!" cried Resurgius.

"Uh-huh. Hell hath no fury, you know," said Mandalay proudly.

Five minutes later Resurgius had Beth arrested and thrown into the old corset room, bound and gagged.

From now on, Resurgius and his Miz Mandalay agreed, she was to have Beth's place in the cup next to Resurgius on the majestic bra.

"O, betrayal!" Resurgius cried, dumping his muscular, plastic buttocks into his cup. "O, treachery!"

"Alas," said Miz Mandalay, climbing into the cup next to his, "you must always remember, my great plastic hero, that hell hath no fury like a Cunnie scorned—and that might one day include me, my love. Circumstances are Fortune, my great muscled Cookie."

12

THE PINAFORE PAPERS

For Resurgius, Beth's attempt to murder him was the last straw.

"This revolution business is too much for me," he said later that night. "I just wish I could go off to the dark side of the moon and lead a quiet, meditative life."

"You're just too tired," Miz Mandalay soothed. "You've been through hell."

"To hell and back," Resurgius sighed stoically.

"My hero," Miz Mandalay commented, squeezing his thigh.

"Mand—may I call you Mandy?"

"Yes, my dear Dong, but how about Amanda, a name I always loved? Isn't it a fairy tale name? Doesn't it mean amorousness, affection, in short, love?"

"Would you consider giving up all this—Amanda—this ugly political life, I mean; this life of political monkeyhood—and running off with me to a desert planet, where it would just be thee and me and the drifting meteorites, the shooting stars?"

"Well, dear Dong, I do so hate to see you give up all that you've fought so hard for in the recent war; but, naturally, my love, whither thou goest, I will go. In the face of love, the life of politics seems but putrid trash. After all, as Jaye Edgahoova might say, politics is nothing but the profound entertainment of the people. I am no longer that interested in entertaining the people. I am in love, and therefore selfish; and perhaps that is the best way to be; to be an individual following his or her bliss. At least, minding my own business, I won't be doing them any harm, poor devils—and let them mind theirs. I often wonder why they do what we tell them to. We are no better than they are. If you cut us, do we not bleed?"

"It's because they're afraid to think for themselves. Because they just mix us up with their ideals."

"It's really quite sad. The herds of beasts must have a leader, I guess."

"Then you'll go with me?"

"Anywhere, anytime."

"Tomorrow morning, to the moon. From there we can get the shuttle on out to Jupiter or Europa."

"It'll be an old-fashioned honeymoon."

"Let's start it tonight. That honeymoon part, I mean."

"Oh, you! Sugarplum."

But in the morning Resurgius had a change of heart. A good night's sleep, prefaced by a vigorous exercise of his sensitized, pumped-up codpiece, had restored his vitality, and once again he felt ready to conquer the Universe.

"I can't give up now," he said to his beloved Amanda, a spoonful of Coco-Puffies at his lips, "I have a responsibility to all the hard-beset Dongs of this world, who look up to me as a symbol."

"That's true, dear," she said. "Now eat your breakfast."

"If I were to quit now it would be like condemning them to another thirty years of slavery."

"It would have that effect."

"But won't you mind not going on our trip to the moon, and then shuttling on to Jupiter or Europa?"

"Resurgius, I knew that you didn't mean what you were saying. You were exhausted."

"I sure was, but I feel great now. Will you help me draw up a plan of action? I don't know how I'm going to do it yet, but I swear I'll think of some way of taking the Univacual Council away from Edgahoova, getting back the Pink House, and putting her on Pluto, where she belongs, just as the French once put Napoleon on Elba in ancient times."

"I'm afraid you might have to wait a while to do that, dear. You have way too few Dongs to your name."

"Can't you—the great Miz Mandalay—go and reclaim your position?"

"You know perfectly well that that's impossible under these present circumstances. Edgahoover's branded me a traitor, publicly, and as long as *she's* the government, her accusation is true. I am a traitor, to *her* government. And don't forget, the Shrike-Troopers are scouring the country for us."

"I guess you're right," said Resurgius. "But there must be some way."

"We'll just have to wait, and build up a new army. My mother used to say that the shortest wait of all, is the wait for stupidity."

"Golly, that's a thought!"

But just then a Dong-trooper came into the padding room where Resurgius and Miz Mandalay were having stirred eggs, having finished their CoCo-Puffies.

"Most General-Admirable Resurgius," he said, "I have been instructed to tell you that big news is exploding all over the Say-screen. I have been instructed to request you to view this news, as it might be of great importance to our cause. Thank you, sir," he said snappily, and left, clicking his worn-down heels.

"What can that be?" said Amanda, tuning in the Say-screen. She got a picture of Sandra Van Orchid, the renowned journalist, then turned up the volume.

Sandra said: "The whole Edgahoova regime has been shaken to its foundations by Daniela Illbird's revelations. Illbird, a member of the staff of the highly secret Strategic Force for Starvation, Death, Destruction and the Atalantic Way, a think tank, has revealed all; admitting that she has been married, illegally, to a Dong for several years. She is quoted as saying, 'I just got sick about what we've been doing to the poor Dongs.' Illbird has also made public many top-secret documents, which she calls the Pinafore Papers. These papers reveal deep and widespread corruption in the government. Surprise! Surprise! Who'd of thunk it?

"One document, a communiqué sent by General Furius to the Pinafore, and marked top-secret, reveals that General Furius' aunt, a Miz named Thickneck, was awarded the sole contract to build The Great Wall of Furius through her niece's instigation. General Furius herself received a considerable rake-off of taxpayer money, and so did our Jaye Edgahoova. Such revelations as this are causing a tremendous public outcry against the current government (there's always another one), which, I hope my viewers will recall, I have always opposed. Mobs are roaming the streets chanting such tags as FRY FURIUS and HANG HOOVA! So far, there has been no comment from the Pink House. But, as I said, it is certain that the government of Jaye Edgahoova has been rocked to its very foundations."

"This is it, Resurgius!" cried Amanda. "This is our *deus ex machina*!

"How?"

"*How*! Oh, I guess Mize think faster than Dongs. Don't you see? The people are ready for us. All we have to do now is to physically assume control. I have a marvelous record as a reformer. I've passed the only liberal legislation in this country since the Great Succession."

"You mean that one that gave all government employees a raise?"

"That one and many others—like the one that requires all Mize who own states to pay at least one bobbit a year in taxes. But never mind that! Stick to the point! I'm a reformer and everyone knows it. It was Edgahoova who blackened my good name, and now that the public knows what she is, they'll love me again, just like always, like Julius Caesar's. I've still got a legal claim to power, and I tell you Atalanta is ready for reform. If I assume power with you at my side, they'll accept you as my co-ruler, I know they will. We'll make it a real heterosexual government. We'll be equal partners!" Her delight compelled her into song:

Mize and Dongs together
Me and Resurgius too—
We'll trip the light fantastic
On you, and you, and you!

"O.K., Amanda, but how'll we get to the Pink House?"

"I've already got that figured out. It's really easy. The balloon you used to kidnap me is still on the roof, isn't it?"

"Yeah. It's deflated, but it only takes a minute to blow it up. But that's not so good;

everybody knows about that balloon now, and Edgahoova's Shrike-Troopers'll be bound to shoot it down as soon as they spot it, and you have to admit that it's pretty noticeable."

"True enough," said Amanda, frowning. Then she grinned. "I've got it! We'll disguise it as an advertisement for that Old Roman Botula Sausage. All we'll need is some brown paint, and maybe a little black for the burnt part."

"Amanda, you're a genius! But how'll we get passed the guards at the Pink House?"

"We only have to worry about the guards on the roof, and I know all of them. They're a great bunch of gals."

"Okay," said Resurgius, "let's fly."

In no time at all, Resurgius, Amanda, three of Resurgius' best Dongs, all former gladiators, and the still bound-and-gagged Beth, were soaring toward Martha, D.C., and the Pink House.

Resurgius' Dongs had done a good job of painting the balloon. It was no longer the same old golden condom, but was now a crisply fried sausage that looked good enough to eat.

"We can be there in about an hour," said Resurgius, "as the sausage flies."

"Oh, Resurgius," Amanda cried, "it's all so thrilling. As soon as we seize power, let's have a darling little Accidental, so that the people can truly think of us as the old fashioned First Family."

"Right, my dear Amanda, but I'll be pretty busy."

"Oh, we can always make time for love—between important meetings, conferences, and things. There are lots of closets."

Resurgius was right, as usual. In less than an hour they came down over the roof of the Pink House. And Amanda was right too, for the guards cheered when they saw her, and cried:

"Miz Mandalay's come home to us!"

"And I'll never leave you again, my darlings," she cried, tears squirting from her plastics and streaming down her cheeks. "And I want you all to meet my Resurgius; he's my Dong."

"Is he safe?" asked one doubtful Shrike.

"He's a good Dong, believe me, dear. Now if you'll excuse us, we have work to do. We are going to fundamentally change this Universe."

Resurgius ordered that Beth be removed from the wicker basket of the balloon and to be brought along. Then the little group descended to the Ovary Office.

They had arrived not a minute too soon.

When they entered the Ovary Office,

they found Edgahoova and Furius desperately packing taxpayer money and treasury plates into two huge trunks.

"Going somewhere?" asked Resurgius.

When Furius saw him, she turned purple, made an animal cry, and charged him. Fortunately, with foresight, and a knowledge of their adversary, all the members of Resurgius' party had taken the precaution of wearing earmuffs, and it was only an earmuff that Furius succeeded in tearing from Resurgius' head. With one powerhouse blow, he succeeded in flooring the unfortunate creature, which he had always wanted to do.

Edgahoova stood aghast.

"You are under arrest in the name of our George Washington," said Resurgius. "Let me warn you that anything you say may be used against you."

"You can't arrest me," said Edgahoova, getting her wits back. *I* am the law."

"Oh no you're not," said Resurgius. "I am!"

"*We* are, dear," put in Amanda.

"You're not," said Edgahoova, "I am."

"Well, there's only one way to settle this," said Resurgius, "and that's with logic." So saying, he stepped up to Edgahoova and drove an iron fist into her belly. She doubled up and sank to the floor. He straightened his hornrims.

"Well, darling," said Amanda, "I guess we know who the law is now, don't we?"

Following Resurgius' orders, the three Dongs assumed supervision over the Pink House staff, and had Edgahoova and Furius thrown into the basement dungeon where taxpayers were often tortured. Edgahoova was placed in the same cell with Old Lynda Johnson, who has been held for many years on charges of war crimes, preferred by one-time philosophess, Bertha Bussle. Upon getting acquainted, they immediately began to twist each other's arms. Poor Old Lynda was really tickled to have an arm to twist, just like the old days. She would have picked Edgahoova up by the ears if she hadn't been so fat. As it was, she did show off her scar.

Almost immediately, Amanda made a request for Say-screen time, and naturally, was granted it. She handled herself admirably, giving the impression that there was nothing more natural than that she should be in command of the government. Not a soul thought to doubt it.

She spoke first, with Resurgius seated beside her.

"Have no fear, my fellow Atalanteans," she said, "the Ship of State is now sailing smoothly, for no one current official has the power to send her from her course. Atalanta shall not fail to carry us forward into a future as yet undreamed, where every soul, like the seed of a great oak, will grow and spread and shut the sun from the ground.

"But the future is here and now. Therefore, my Atalanteans, I officially proclaim this day, Mae 25, 3000, as Equality Day. From this day forth, Dongs are recognized as full citizens of Atalanta, with all the rights and privileges thereof.

"And now, I should like to introduce you to the new Co-leader of Atalanta, the great General-Admirable Resurgius, former leader of the Dongs!"

"I only wish to say, on this solemn occasion" said Resurgius, "that I'll work with Miz Mandalay, to me, Amanda, here to do my best to bring all of you together and to heal the wounds inflicted by the late civil war. I hope to be the leader of *all* the people, not just the ones I like. And I promise you that I'll do everything I can to please every one of you out there, with charity for all. I thank you."

After their speeches, Resurgius and his Amanda waited in front of the Say-screen to see if the reviews would be good or bad.

Sandra Van Orchid, the first to comment, said, "Let's give these two fighting liberals a chance."

Norma Postman said: "I'd like to debate Resurgius. He's got some interesting ideas."

Petite Hannabelle said: "They're gutsy!"

Generally, the reviews were very good, and the general public took the attractive young couple to its heart. It was Camelotian.

In short, they were in like Flynne.

13

THE NEW ORDER

In the first months of Resurgius' and Amanda's Co-leadership, they pleased the public by instituting many reforms, such as warning the school crossing guards about taking the children's' lunch money, and preventing the Old Roman Botula Sausage Company from stuffing their product with cow dung.

Actually, Resurgius left most of the administrative duties to Amanda, now affectionately known to the public as Handy Mandy. He had bigger fish to fry.

Most of his first days in office were spent in coming to terms with the Space-Pirates. He was now in a much better position to bargain with Blackbeard than he had been at the time of their last meeting, and could truthfully claim that she and her Space-Pirates had done very little to help his cause.

On the other hand, Blackbeard still had a copy of their written agreement, which he had signed when he was at a low point, and which, if made public—Resurgius shuddered to think of the consequences. Besides which, Blackbeard had begun to harass his government with small space snarls. She really did own him, lock, stock, and barrel.

"Well," Resurgius thought philosophically, "was there ever a political leader who wasn't owned by someone?" Finally, he acceded to every one of Blackbeard's original demands.

"After all," he consoled himself, "it's the taxpayers' money, not mine." But he thought, too, "it could have been honest, though."

One of Blackbeard's original demands had been that Resurgius keep the war on the dark side of the moon going, so that her cousin, the banker, might take over the Offence Industries, ownership of which in her cousin's name was another of her demands, so that he, the cousin, might supply bombs and rockets for the war. This meant that Resurgius was forced, eventually, to enact new draft laws, for the army was running low again on soldiers. Also, it was troublesome having to dream up circumstances which could be used to explain Atalanta's continued involvement there.

He was also responsible for punishing the guilty and rewarding the innocent. Publia he had arrested and thrown into the dungeon with Edgahoova and Furius. Claudia he pardoned, for, as we have mentioned, she married the village smithy. Cossina, who had defected to his side during the war, he welcomed back to Martha, D.C., with a triumphal parade, awarded her the Atalanta Shtick, highest of all medals, and made her Chief of Staff, all of which goes to show that the difference between a dirty traitor and an illustrious hero is just the difference between winding up on the losing or on the winning side.

On June 25, 3000, Edgahoova and Furius tried to escape, Edgahoova succeeding and Furius wounded in the attempt. What had happened was that Furius had called her naive young guard over and asked if she might whisper something in her ear. The poor Cunnie put her ear to Furius' mouth and found herself to be captive. Furius forced her to unlock her cell, then to free Edgahoova.

Apparently, there was an argument about taking Miz Bet along, which argument Furius won, convincing Edgahoova that she could not trust Miz Bet. But the ensuing argument had wasted precious minutes. Several more guards had entered the cell block. While Furius went after these newcomers, Edgahoova slipped away. She has not been seen or heard of since, but for the persistent rumor that she is the mysterious leader of the Vigilante Libs, a radical political group based on the dark side of the moon.

As for Furius, this first attempt failing, she tried again that same day to escape, and this time was killed in the attempt, falling off her famous Brahma rocket nicknamed "Bull." The rocket itself had been bent clean in half due to her weight and clutching legs, and is now in a museum to show what happens to evil-doers: they spin in circles forever—unless they fall off.

Publia was brought to trial, and through the influence of Blackbeard, who was her second cousin once removed, she was given a suspended sentence on her charge of treason.

"All's well that ends well," she was heard to comment. Upon her release, she went back into show biz, which, if you'll remember, had been her first love, taking a job as a Dong impersonator in an All-Night Club.

14

RESURGIUS IN LOVE

Resurgius had only one last problem, and that was the question of how, what had come to be known as "L'affaire Bet" by the public, should be handled.

Amanda had become an awful pest about this situation, for it was her most ardent desire that she and Resurgius should be married, that venerable institution now having been given once again the sanction of law. She wanted them to be the first First Family of the New

Order, but how could this be done so long as Beth kept insisting from her cell in the Pink House dungeon that she was actually the wife of Resurgius, and therefore the First Lady of the Land?

Resurgius cursed himself for ever having married her. He had only done so because she had made him feel such gratitude toward her and had told him that it was love. Now, through Amanda's offices, he knew better. Desperate, he summoned his top legal advisor, Attorney General Mitch Shyster, and his top spiritual advisor, Reverend Billy Cracker.

"What shall I do?" he asked of them.

Attorney General Shyster replied:

"The marriage wasn't legal in the first place, for there was a specific law against the institution of marriage at that time, and, frankly, I sometimes wish you hadn't countermanded it."

"All right," said Resurgius, searching his conscience, "perhaps it wasn't legal in the eyes of the Law, but what about in the eyes of the Lord?"

"Ah kin only ahdvise yo, suh," said the Reverend Billy, "ta search out yo conscience. When yo sayed 'I do' didja mean it, or was yo bein' misguided by thah forces of Evil?"

"I think I was being misguided."

"Then they is no marriage."

"Golly, thanks a lot fellows—this is a big great day for yours truly," said Resurgius. "But I'm still going to have to get rid of Beth or she'll always be in my hair."

"Let yo conscience be yo guide, my son," said the Reverend Billy.

The next day, Resurgius brought charges against Beth. He charged her with treason against the former government. Her large epaulettes were torn from her shoulders and recycled into heavy-duty mops. She was then exiled to Pluto, much as Napoleon had been exiled to Elba, to live a life of contemplation and regret.

Resurgius and his Amanda enjoyed their nuptials later the same afternoon.

Both died in office, Resurgius first, unfortunately, of toxic masculinity caused by his plastic muscle-suit with the big "R" on its chest, which turned out to be poisonous—and at his state funeral all that was left to observe was his skinny little body, his big head with its shock of auburn hair, his huge horn-rimmed, thick-lensed spectacles, and a wan smile of victory. He had a right to his rictus, having put Dongs in their rightful place.

The beautifully embosomed Amanda died some twenty years later, having enjoyed over two decades of a smashing superduper Univacual high life.

Milton Keynes UK
Ingram Content Group UK Ltd.
UKHW020331060724
445023UK00012BB/146/J